PATTERNS OF GLORY

STUDIES IN CHARLES WILLIAMS

STEPHEN BARBER

Apocryphile Press
PO Box 255
Hannacroix, NY 12087
www.apocryphilepress.com

Copyright © 2024 by Stephen Barber
Printed in the United States of America
ISBN 978-1-958061-90-9 | paper
ISBN 978-1-958061-91-6 | ePub

No part of this book may be reproduced, stored in a retrieval system, or transmitted in any form or by any means—electronic, mechanical, photocopy, recording, or otherwise —without written permission of the author and publisher, except for brief quotations in printed reviews.

Please join our mailing list at www.apocryphilepress.com/free. We'll keep you up-to- date on all our new releases, and we'll also send you a FREE BOOK. Visit us today!

For Marushka
who does not care for Charles Williams
and for Grevel
who does

PREFACE

This is a collection of my scattered articles about Charles Williams and, in particular, about the Taliessin poems. They were written over a period of many years in the intervals of a busy life largely spent doing quite different things, but they have been welcomed by those who share my fascination with Williams and who, I hope, will find it convenient to have them gathered together.

Williams does not appear on many university or college reading lists, and most of those who come to take an interest in him do so from reading three other writers, all of whom were friends of his: T. S. Eliot, Tolkien and C. S. Lewis. My introduction was rather different. When I was a teenager, I went to stay a few days with the boy who had been my best friend at primary school. While there, his mother lent me a book by a writer she admired and whom she had known personally. The book was *Many Dimensions,* and the writer was Charles Williams, of whom I had not previously heard. My friend's mother was Alice Mary Hadfield, Williams's first biographer.

This planted a seed which took some years to germinate. During my student years I saw and bought copies of Williams's two cycles of Arthurian poems, *Taliessin through Logres* and *The Region of the Summer Stars*, together with what remains the best introduction to them: *Arthurian Torso*, consisting of Williams's unfinished study of the Arthurian legend, *The Figure of Arthur*, and C. S. Lewis's exposition of Williams's poems. These fascinated me and continue to do so: I am one of those who consider that they are his best work, as indeed he wanted them to be considered. I also read the remaining novels, the plays and his critical and theological prose. I was drawn by the incantatory power of the best of his poetry, the mystery evoked so powerfully by it, the reformulation and representation of Christian ideas in a different terminology and the constant awareness of an unseen spiritual world.

Later, I joined the Charles Williams Society, which flourished for about forty years, and was its treasurer for the last dozen of them. They commissioned my first review, of Thomas Howard's book on the novels, which is much the oldest piece here. In the intervals between other projects, I wrote many of the remaining pieces, which the Society always welcomed warmly and readily, for which I remain most grateful.

I have arranged these essays in a thematic, not a chronological order. I begin with the one on Williams and T. S. Eliot, as it offers an oversight of Williams's career, compared with that of his contemporary, friend and, indeed, rival, Eliot. For my generation Eliot was the undisputed literary arbiter for poetry, a successor in role to Ben Jonson, Dryden, Dr Johnson, Coleridge and Arnold. I do not think that anyone since has yet assumed the mantle which Eliot had in his heyday. This essay is followed by 'Alternative history and symbolic geography in the Taliessin poems.' This was commissioned for an anthology of essays on 'impossible geographies,' which never appeared. I took the opportunity to set out the historical and geographical background to the Taliessin poems, as I thought Lewis had rather ducked this in *Arthurian Torso*. The essay on 'Metaphysical and romantic' takes up a suggestive comment by Lewis on Williams's idiom and explores a characteristic poetic strategy of his. There follow several short pieces on aspects of these poems, a review of two books on the Holy Grail and two other topics. 'People and Places' is not an essay but a reference guide, compiled when I had thoughts of preparing an annotated critical edition of the Taliessin poems. To this section also belongs the note on the text. (I was pleased to see that a recent reprint of the poems adopted my textual suggestions.)

The remaining articles move away from the poems. I have not written at length about the novels, but my review of Thomas Howard's book on them is a proxy for this. I have in, general, eschewed writing about Williams's personal life, which has been so thoroughly explored by Grevel Lindop in his biography; the piece on Williams as a father was written for a symposium on this biography. 'Williams as a literary critic' offers an overview of Williams's work in this field. The review of the book on Williams and Lewis is a kind of complement to that on Williams and Eliot. That on Williams and Dante studies aims to situate his work among that of other readers and translators of Dante at the time. As both these last two pieces necessarily give a good deal of space to Dante, I thought I would finish with a short piece directly about Dante, which makes incidental reference to Williams.

There are two other pieces which I cannot include, since I never got round to writing them up. One would have been on mathematical imagery in the Taliessin poems. The main point would have been that Williams saw theology as an exact science, for which mathematics was the closest analogy. So, the 'trigonometrical milk of doctrine' (which has baffled some readers of 'The Vision of the Empire') is milk, as it is in the New Testament, but trigonometrical in honour of the Trinity and of this mathematical analogy. The fact that mathematics can also treat of infinite series and lines meeting at infinity, as in 'The Sister of Percivale,' also makes it a suitable metaphor for divine qualities.

The other unwritten piece would have explored whether Williams's Way of Affirmation of images was a Platonic ascent. Plato in the *Symposium* expounds how the love of an individual person can lead through a process of discipline to the love of absolute beauty, divorced from any one individual. Williams follows Dante in thinking that the ascent can be made without relinquishing the love of an individual, a belief also championed by Renaissance writers such as Ficino.

My title is taken from a statement by Williams I have always found arresting: 'The word glory, to English ears, usually means no more than a kind of mazy bright blur. But the maze should be, though generally it is not, exact, and the brightness should be that of a geometrical pattern.'

It remains to say that many of these pieces have benefited from the comments of my friends, who include Dr Brian Horne, Dr Sørina Higgins, Professor Emeritus Grevel Lindop, Dr Richard Sturch and others. I have made some revisions, mostly to regularise the references, which are given afresh in each essay; there is no separate bibliography. I have not been able to eliminate all repetitions. I have done some updating, chiefly in the first essay, where Eliot's letters to Emily Hale were published after its first appearance.

Stephen Barber
February 2024

CONTENTS

Map for Taliessin Poems	x
Charles Williams and T. S. Eliot: Friends and Rivals	1
Alternative History and Symbolic Geography in the Taliessin Poems	21
Metaphysical and Romantic in the Taliessin Poems	33
Two Books on the Holy Grail	57
Heraclitus on the Way of Exchange	61
Williams and the Sea Nymph	69
A Debt to George Eliot?	75
People and Places in the Taliessin Poems	77
A Note on the Text of the Taliessin Poems	91
Thomas Howard on the Novels	95
Charles Williams as a Father	99
Charles Williams as a Literary Critic	103
Williams and Lewis on Co-inherence	135
Charles Williams and Dante Studies in England in the Twentieth Century	139
The Reunion of Dante and Beatrice	151
Sources and Acknowledgements	155

Map for Taliessin poems.

CHARLES WILLIAMS AND T. S. ELIOT: FRIENDS AND RIVALS

We tend to think of Williams's principal literary friendships as being with the Inklings in general and with C. S. Lewis in particular. Lewis's role in obtaining lecturing and tutoring work for Williams in wartime Oxford and in expounding his Arthurian poems in 'Williams and the Arthuriad'[1] cannot be overestimated, but a longer and arguably even deeper literary friendship was that of Williams with T. S. Eliot.

They first met in late 1933 or 1934[2] through the good offices of Lady Ottoline Morrell, who held a literary salon to which she invited writers of the day. It is worth taking stock of where they each were in their literary careers at that point. They were close in age, Williams having been born in 1886 and Eliot in 1888, and there were both remarkable similarities and remarkable differences between their respective positions.[3]

Each of them had a day job in publishing, Williams with the London branch of the Oxford

---

1. The second part of Charles Williams and C. S Lewis, *Arthurian Torso: containing the posthumous fragment of 'The Figure of Arthur' by Charles Williams and a Commentary on the Arthurian poems of Charles Williams by C. S. Lewis* (Oxford: Oxford University Press, 1948).
2. Eliot said it was 'in the late 'twenties, I think,' Introduction to *All Hallows Eve* (New York: Pellegrini and Cudahy, 1948) but Grevel Lindop has established that it was in fact not before late 1933, 'Charles Williams and W. B. Yeats,' in Warwick Gould (ed.), *Yeats Annual No. 21: Yeats's Legacies*, (Cambridge: Open Book Publishers, 2018). They certainly met on 29 September 1934, but that was probably not their first meeting.
3. Biographical details without further note are taken, for Eliot from Lyndall Gordon, *T. S. Eliot: An Imperfect Life* (New York: W. W. Norton, 1999) and *The Hyacinth Girl: T. S. Eliot's Hidden Muse* (London: Virago Press, 2022), and Robert Crawford: *Young Eliot: from St. Louis to 'The Waste Land'* and *Eliot after 'The Waste Land,'* (London: Jonathan Cape, 2015 and 2022); and for Williams from A. M. Hadfield, *An Introduction to Charles Williams* (London: Robert Hale, 1959), and *Charles Williams: An Exploration of his Life and Work* (New York: Oxford University Press, 1983), and from Grevel Lindop, *Charles Williams: The Third Inkling* (London: Oxford University Press, 2015).

University Press (OUP), Eliot with Faber and Faber. Each had a boss who was a literary man, who had been a fellow of All Souls College in Oxford, who wrote books of their own and who had edited standard editions of English poets: Williams's boss, Sir Humphrey Milford, had edited Cowper and Leigh Hunt; Geoffrey Faber, Eliot's boss, had edited John Gay. Neither Williams nor Eliot was an academic, but each had taught evening classes. Both had published a good deal of poetry, Williams more than Eliot. Both also wrote plays. They had each done a fair amount of related literary work, though Williams had carried out more editing of anthologies and Eliot more journalism. They were both committed Anglican Christians, attached to the Anglo-Catholic wing of the Church of England, though they were both also attracted by the theology of Karl Barth, who was from the Reformed tradition.[4] They shared a preoccupation with the relationship between spirit and matter. Their literary enthusiasms included, in addition to English writers, Virgil and, especially, Dante, on whom they would each write a book. Both admired Malory and explored the possible esoteric significance of the Grail legends, Williams through A. E. Waite,[5] Eliot through Jessie Weston.[6] They both admired Dickens and enjoyed detective stories. On the darker side, each had a troubled marriage and had an idealized other woman in their lives, Phyllis Jones for Williams, Emily Hale for Eliot. And each had an interest in the occult, though Williams went farther than Eliot. He had been a practising member of at least one and possibly two occult organizations and drew on this in much of his writing. Eliot had shown an interest in the Gurdjieff-Ouspensky movement;[7] he published Owen Barfield, later an occasional Inkling, who was a follower of Rudolf Steiner's anthroposophy. He also published *An Adventure*, about an apparent time-slip experience at the Petit Trianon, and the works of J. W. Dunne dealing with precognition.[8] And he enjoyed the occult themes in Williams's novels, which we shall come to.

---

4. Eliot: see notes at *The Poems of T. S. Eliot* ed. Christopher Ricks and Jim McCue (London: Faber, 2016), 2 vols., I. 826-7, 956, 985. Williams chose a number of passages from Barth in his two religious anthologies, *The Passion of Christ* (Oxford: Oxford University Press, 1939) and *The New Christian Year* (Oxford: Oxford University Press, 1941). For both of them the work cited was Barth's influential commentary *The Epistle to the Romans*, translated E. C. Hoskyns (Oxford: Oxford University Press, 1933).
5. A. E. Waite, *The Hidden Church of the Holy Graal: its legends and symbolism*, (London: Redman, 1909). See Hadfield, *Exploration*, 24. There is no evidence that Williams read Waite's later expansion of this book, *The Holy Grail* (London: Rider, 1933).
6. Jessie L. Weston, *From Ritual to Romance* (Cambridge: Cambridge University Press, 1920). See Eliot's Notes to *The Waste Land* and *The Poems*, I. 588-91.
7. For details see Paul Murray, *T. S. Eliot and Mysticism: the Secret History of 'Four Quartets'* (London: Macmillan Press, 1991), 167-70.
8. C. A. E. Moberly and E. F. Jourdain, *An Adventure*, fourth edition (London: Faber, 1931); J. W Dunne, *An Experiment with Time*, new edition (London: Faber, 1934). Both works were taken over from previous publishers. Faber went on to publish Dunne's later books. *An Adventure* gives an account by two women who visited Versailles in the early twentieth century and appeared to find themselves back in the eighteenth; Dunne explores the possibility of dreams of precognition, which appear to show that the future can be already knowable. The two taken together

However, in examining these similarities, remarkable differences open up. Each had jobs in London, but Williams had lived in London or nearby St Albans's all his life; Eliot was an immigrant from the United States who had taken British citizenship a few years before. Williams had grown up in humble circumstances, had known poverty and had been unable to complete his university degree because of lack of funds. Eliot had had a privileged upbringing in St. Louis, with summer holidays in a second home in New England. He had been supported by his family through not only a first degree but a considerable period of postgraduate study in Paris, Munich and Oxford. He had written a doctoral thesis and could have had an academic career if he had wanted it. Both worked in publishing, but Eliot had been parachuted in as a director because of his financial as well as his literary acumen; Williams, on the other hand, had worked his way up and was never on the board at OUP. Williams's poetry had won little recognition, but Eliot had achieved fame in 1922 with *The Waste Land* and was recognized as a leading modernist along with his mentor Ezra Pound and their friend James Joyce. Thanks not only to his poetry, but also through critical works beginning with *The Sacred Wood* (1920), articles, reviews and editing *The Criterion*, and also through the patronage he could offer younger poets, such as W. H. Auden, at Faber Eliot had also consolidated his position as a literary arbiter, which he was to retain for the rest of his life. Williams had no such standing, though he was arguably the more versatile, as he wrote novels and biographies, neither of which Eliot attempted.

In their spiritual life, Williams was a cradle Anglican whereas Eliot was born a Unitarian, lapsed from this and had become an Anglican convert. Spiritually, Eliot was drawn to the negative way expounded by mystics, whereas Williams developed a Romantic Theology, later subsumed into his Way of Affirmation, on which more later. Their literary tastes also diverged in some cases: Williams greatly admired Milton, also Wordsworth and the Romantic poets; Eliot was equivocal about Milton—he was credited by Leavis with effecting Milton's 'dislodgement'[9]—and once dismissed the Romantics as 'poets of assured though modest merit.'[10] The two men's marriages led in different directions: Eliot separated from Vivien, his wife, whereas Williams's marriage to Florence survived. In relation to the occult, Williams

---

suggest that time is an illusion. The lines 'If all time is eternally present,' *Burnt Norton* I. 4, and 'the loop in time', *The Family Reunion*, Part I. Scene 1, 134, derive from these ideas.

9. F. R. Leavis, *Revaluation* (Harmondsworth: Penguin 1964), 42. First published in 1936. This was written before Eliot's 1936 essay on Milton, 'Milton I' in *On Poetry and Poets* (London: Faber, 1957), which is more nuanced than Leavis anticipated. There is a full discussion of the controversy over Milton, including the contributions of Leavis, Eliot and Williams, in Christopher Ricks, *Milton's Grand Style* (Oxford: Oxford University Press, 1963). See also the discussion below.

10. Eliot, 'Observations', *The Egoist*, 5 (May 1918), 69; *The Complete Prose of T. S. Eliot: The Critical Edition*, ed. Ronald Schuchard and others (Baltimore: Johns Hopkins University Press, 8 vols. 2014-9), I. 711. Uncollected essays of Eliot are quoted from this edition..

was to draw on this extensively in his novels and, to a certain extent, in his poetry, whereas Eliot's public attitude was usually that of amused dabbling.[11]

Before their meeting Eliot had already made an impression on Williams. His essay on Eliot in his 1930 critical study *Poetry at Present* shows him struggling with Eliot's poetry; Williams himself admitted that the essay was unsatisfactory. However, I consider that reading *The Waste Land*, which draws on the Arthurian legends, led Williams gradually to rethink his own plans for a long poem or poems dealing with them. Eliot's poem had made the older kind of narrative poem, as exemplified by Tennyson's *Idylls of the King*, seem hopelessly old-fashioned. The key new feature was the suppression of connecting narrative, what Eliot called the 'links in the chain,'[12] in favour of the imagist method, a succession of vivid scenes without linking narrative or explanation, whose dramatic character has often been remarked. This was to be Williams's technique in *Thomas Cranmer of Canterbury* and *Taliessin through Logres*. (In *The Region of the Summer Stars* Williams returns to verse narrative, but rethought after the experience of dispensing with it.)

Then Eliot had adopted from Joyce's *Ulysses* what he called the 'mythical method,' of which he said:

> Mr Joyce's parallel use of the *Odyssey* has a great importance. It has the importance of a scientific discovery ... In using the myth, in manipulating a continuous parallel between contemporaneity and antiquity, Mr Joyce is pursuing a method which others must pursue after him ... Instead of narrative method, we may now use the mythical method.[13]

It does not seem as if Williams ever read *Ulysses* for himself, but Eliot's counterpointing of different historical periods against the present day in *The Waste Land*, in his own application of the mythical method, may have suggested to Williams the technique of his earlier novels. In these, a magical practice or object from the world of myth and his occult studies is brought into the contemporary world: magic in *Shadows of Ecstasy*, the Holy Grail—also a theme in *The Waste Land*—in *War in Heaven*, the philosopher's stone in *Many Dimensions*, the Platonic archetypes in *The Place of the Lion*, and the Tarot pack in *The Greater Trumps*. He also used the 'mythical method' in the play *Seed of Adam*. It may also have encouraged the creative use of anachronism which he was to adopt in his Arthurian poems.[14]

---

11. See the Madame Sosostris passage in *The Waste Land*, I. 43-59, the fortune-telling passage in *The Dry Salvages*, V. 1-15, and, for Eliot's general attitude to the occult, his reader's report quoted at *The Poems*, I. 983.
12. Eliot, Preface to St.-John Perse, *Anabase*, *The Poems*, II. 132.
13. Eliot, '*Ulysses*, Order and Myth,' *The Dial*, November 1923; *Complete Prose*, III. 476-9.
14. I explore this further in my article, 'Alternative History and Symbolic Geography on the background to the Arthurian poems.'

To conclude on the influence of *The Waste Land*, Williams would have been struck by the role the blind Greek seer Tiresias plays in it. Eliot said in a note:

> Tiresias, though a mere spectator and not indeed a character, is yet the most important personage in the poem ... What Tiresias sees, in fact, is the substance of the poem.[15]

Williams was to give Taliessin the same function in his own Arthurian poems, and this was to provide the unifying device he needed. The Skeleton in *Thomas Cranmer of Canterbury* and the Accuser in *Judgement at Chelmsford* perform similar functions.

Before that first meeting they had some exchanges by letter, mainly on publishing issues, but Eliot expressed appreciation of Williams's essay on him in *Poetry at Present*—the same one which Williams was disappointed by—and of his play *A Myth of Shakespeare*.[16] Then in 1930 Eliot published *Ash Wednesday*. Section II has a famously riddling opening:

> Lady, three white leopards sat under a juniper tree
> In the cool of the day, having fed to satiety
> On my legs my heart my liver and that which had been contained
> In the hollow round of my skull.

And Section IV contains the passage:

> Redeem
> The unread vision in the higher dream
> While jewelled unicorns draw by the gilded hearse.

Williams read the poem with his colleagues at work and wrote to Eliot on 17 May, first thanking him for his Introduction to G. Wilson Knight's *The Wheel of Fire*, which his colleague Gerard Hopkins had commissioned from him, and then praising *Ash Wednesday*:

---

15. Eliot, *The Waste Land*, note to line 218.
16. Eliot to Williams, 2 April 1929 and 5 October 1929, *The Letters of T. S. Eliot*, ed. Valerie Eliot and John Haffenden, seven vols. to date (London: Faber, 2009 in progress), IV, 472, 626-7. (This edition has so far reached the end of 1941; later letters are cited from various sources.) The letters to Emily Hale have been published separately online at https://tseliot.com/the-eliot-hale-letters/indexterms #abbey_of_-st_mary_the_virgin_burnham, no page numbers, accessed 30 January 2024. These are the first (extant) letters from Eliot to Williams. In 1925 Williams had submitted his *Outlines of Romantic Theology* to Faber & Gwyer, predecessors of Faber & Faber, where it was considered by Osbert Burdett but eventually not published. Eliot had only just joined the firm and seems to have had no involvement with this; A. M. Hadfield, Introduction to Williams, *Outlines of Romantic Theology* (Grand Rapids: Eerdmans, 1990), xiii; Lindop, *Charles Williams*, 121-2, 143.

> It will not perhaps displease you to know that Mr Milford and Hopkins and I all, separately and together, agreed that it seemed to suggest to us that our great-grandchildren would find it great poetry; but that by the way. Without asking for meaning or interpretation or anything, it did just occur to us to wonder whether there were any,—well, say, allusion—in the "three white leopards" or the "unicorns dragging a gilded hearse," that one would perhaps be happier for recognizing. Dante or "the Forest Philosophers of India" (my God!) or anything? . . . (We have looked at Dante, but unachievingly.)[17]

The reference to 'the Forest Philosophers of India' is a piece of gentle flattery, as Eliot had used the phrase in his Introduction to Wilson Knight's book.[18]

Eliot replied on 22 May:

> But if one can explain *obscurus* by *obscurior*, and the less by the greater, the *Vita Nuova* may help. If the three leopards or the unicorn contain any allusions literary, I don't know what they are. Can't I sometimes invent nonsense, instead of always being supposed to borrow it?[19]

As explication this was not very helpful—Eliot told other correspondents that the leopards represented the world, the flesh and the devil[20]—but its relaxed tone confirms a friendly relationship, although at that stage only by correspondence.

Following that first meeting Eliot read *War in Heaven* and *The Place of the Lion* at the instigation of Lady Ottoline Morrell.[21] Thereafter he read the novels as they came out or soon afterwards, or, in the case of the last two, *Descent into Hell* and *All Hallows Eve*, before they came out, as he published them. From then on Eliot and Williams continued to be in contact, meeting more frequently as time went on until the war.

Also from that time we can start to see influences between them, going both ways. The first to show this was Williams's novel *The Greater Trumps*, of 1932. This dealt with the Tarot cards, which became part of the equipment of those practising ritual magic in the nineteenth century.[22] Williams possessed his own pack, whereas Eliot, despite drawing on it in *The Waste*

---

17. Hadfield, *Exploration*, 79.
18. G. Wilson Knight, *The Wheel of Fire: Interpretations of Shakespearean Tragedy* (London: Oxford University Press, 1930), xvi; *Complete Prose* IV, 147. Eliot had studied Indian philosophy at Harvard.
19. Eliot to Williams, 22 May 1930; *Letters*, V, 196-7; *The Poems* I. 741-2.
20. *The Poems*, I. 730, 742, 750. There is no single source for the jewelled unicorns. Eliot also said that much of the imagery came out of dreams.
21. He actually said that these were Williams's first two novels (Introduction to *All Hallows Eve*). In fact, although *The Place of the Lion* and *Many Dimensions* were both published in the same year, 1931, *Many Dimensions* was published in January and *The Place of the Lion* in September. The first written of the novels, *Shadows of Ecstasy*, was only published after the next four. Eliot wrote appreciatively to Williams about *War in Heaven* and *The Place of the Lion*, Eliot to Williams, 7 October 1934; *Letters*, VII, 337-8,
22. Ronald Decker, Thierry Depaulis and Michael Dummett, *A Wicked Pack of Cards: The Origins of the Occult Tarot*

Land, had in fact only once seen a pack and admitted being unfamiliar with its constitution.[23] The Greater Trumps take their name from the twenty cards additional to the ordinary playing cards, the so-called Major Arcana, which in the novel Williams postulated derived from a set of gold figurines which were passed on in a secret tradition—the Tarot originals, an invention by him. These appeared to be in a continual dance, apart from the Fool at the centre, which appeared not to move. Only Sibyl, aptly named, sees the Fool moving and so completing the pattern.[24]

Williams sent Eliot a copy of the novel, and he wrote in reply:

> You know that I enjoy everything you do in this kind, and only clamour for more. It is a thing that nobody else, so far as I know, can do at all.

However, he had reservations; in particular:

> I was not either very credulous or deeply impressed by the dancing figures, although the idea behind them is a good one.[25]

Nevertheless, in 1935 Eliot wrote *Burnt Norton*, and in Section II we read:

> At the still point of the turning world. Neither flesh nor fleshless;
> Neither from nor towards; at the still point, there the dance is,
> But neither arrest nor movement.

The still point itself is from Barth,[26] but the dance, as Eliot acknowledged, is taken from *The Greater Trumps*.[27]

Also in 1935, Williams asked Eliot for help with *The New Book of English Verse*, an anthology of older English poets he was compiling as a freelance for Victor Gollancz. Eliot gave him some suggestions but refused to let Williams include his name, along with others, as Associate Editor. The issue was resolved amicably, and Eliot later commended the antholo-

---

(New York: St. Martin's Press, 1996). The successor work by Decker and Dummett, *A History of the Occult Tarot 1870-1970* (London: Duckworth, 2002), has brief references to Williams's *The Greater Trumps*, 310, 311.
23. Eliot's note to *The Waste Land I: The Burial of the Dead*, 46, and several remarks reported at *The Poems*, I, 610.
24. Williams, *The Greater Trumps* (London: Faber, 1954), 28, 73-4. First published 1932.
25. Eliot to Williams, letter of 24 January 1935; *Letters*, VII. 487-8.
26. Note 4 above.
27. Both Williams and Eliot confirmed this to Helen Gardner, *The Composition of Four Quartets* (London: Faber, 1978), 85, and *The Poems*, I. 916. Stephen Medcalf argues for a wider influence of Williams both on *Burnt Norton* and on Eliot more generally, 'The Dance along the artery—T. S. Eliot and Charles Williams,' *The Charles Williams Society Newsletter*, no. 100, Autumn 2001, 10-47.

gy.²⁸ As publishers they were also at the same time rivals, each engaged in producing an anthology of modern poetry. Williams's superiors at the Oxford University Press wanted a prominent poet to edit theirs; they settled on W. B. Yeats, whose choices were eccentric and idiosyncratic.²⁹ The resulting *Oxford Book of Modern Verse* was a disaster; W. H. Auden suggested it was 'the most deplorable volume ever issued under the imprint of that highly respected firm.'³⁰ Eliot, on the other hand, chose as his editor Michael Roberts, whose ability as an anthologist had already been demonstrated.³¹ The *Faber Book of Modern Verse* formed the taste of a generation, was frequently reprinted and three times revised.

They wrote plays for the Canterbury Festival in successive years: Eliot's *Murder in the Cathedral* in 1935, and Williams's *Thomas Cranmer of Canterbury* in 1936. Both were commissioned by Bishop George Bell, were directed by E. Martin Browne and had Robert Speaight in the leading roles.³² I have wondered whether Williams's setting his Grail quest in a contemporary setting in *War in Heaven*, together with Kenneth Mornington's exhortation 'Better be modern than minor,'³³ might have encouraged Eliot to write the scene in *Murder in the Cathedral* where the four knights address the audience to justify the murder in modern terms.³⁴ On *Cranmer*, Eliot wrote to Williams: 'you have chosen a more difficult subject than mine;'³⁵ he attended the first performance and wrote appreciatively to Williams about the play.³⁶ He gave his impression of Williams and his play at the time to Emily Hale:

> We went in to the Royal Fountain Hotel first, to greet the author, Charles Williams, whom I have known off and on for some years: a queer, likeable, rather pathetic fellow, a very humble person, very radiant and excited over it all, and the prospect of being presented to the Archbishop. The play is very good, I think: though the verse is only first-rate journeyman's work, it is quite fresh

---

28. Charles Williams (ed.), *The New Book of English Verse* (London: Gollancz, 1935); Eliot *Letters* VII. 689-90, 729-30; 'What is minor poetry?', *On Poetry and Poets*, 43 (it is also possible, but less likely, that Eliot was here referring to Williams's earlier anthology, *Victorian Narrative Verse* (Oxford: Clarendon Press, 1927)).
29. Lindop, *Charles Williams*, 234.
30. W. H. Auden. 'The Public v. the Late Mr William Butler Yeats,' *Partisan Review*, Spring 1939; *The English Auden* ed. Edward Mendelson (London: Faber, 1977), 390.
31. His anthologies *New Signatures* (London: Hogarth Press, 1932), and *New Country* (London: Hogarth Press, 1933), had introduced the Auden generation to a wider audience. For Eliot's comments on the *Faber Book*, see *The Poems* I. 1224-5.
32. For the background see Kenneth Pickering, *Drama in the Cathedral*, second edition (Colwall: J. Garnet Miller, 2001).
33. *War in Heaven* (London: Faber, 1954), 96. First published 1930.
34. Eliot said much later that this might have been suggested by Bernard Shaw's *Saint Joan*, 'Poetry and Drama,' *On Poetry and Poets*, 81.
35. Eliot to Williams, 10 September 1935; *Letters*, VII. 747.
36. Eliot to Williams, 6 July 1936; *Letters* VIII 252-3.

and good; and though there is no plot beyond a sequence of events and very little action or really dramatic dialogue, the final impression of Cranmer going off to be burnt was very intense.[37]

Eliot was to change his mind about Williams's social skills, as I shall show later. It was during this period that Williams wrote to Eliot, following one of their meetings: 'I have not known so happy and easy a time since the dearest of my male friends died two years ago.'[38]

Another point of contact between them began at around this time. Williams had been friends with Anne Bradby, later Ridler, since 1930.[39] She was Humphrey Milford's niece. In 1936 she started working for Faber and was Eliot's secretary 1935-40.[40] Her autobiography contains many reminiscences of both men but none of their interaction.[41]

A charming incident not long after demonstrates how Williams handled Eliot's greater fame and shows both men at their most attractive. It arose from a performance in March 1937, not of *Cranmer*, but of William's earlier play *The Rite of the Passion*. Following this Williams wrote an occasional poem, which he later sent to Eliot, saying 'The joyous fact is that it records an actual incident.' A 'elderlyish' woman at his play had accosted him:

> Presently she said: "Do you know Mr. Eliot?"
> I said: "Yes.'
> More minutes went by; we still gazed—
> I gravely now, partly out of respect to Mr Eliot,
> partly in my own patience, partly to play up to her.
> Presently she said: "do you know *Murder in the Cathedral?*"
> I said: "Yes."
> Time slipped into a crack and slept and came back.
> She said: "I think that's a very fine play."
> (No emphasis, no hostility, nothing, a mere fact discovered in a voice.) I
>   said; "yes."
> She looked at me again for some time and then went away.
> That was all. As I say
> against bitterness I am always on guard but I *do* think it hard.[42]

---

37. Eliot, letter to Emily Hale, 22 June 1936.
38. Williams to Eliot, 21 November, 1935, quoted by Hadfield, *Exploration*, 128. The reference was to Daniel Nicholson, whom Williams had known since 1915.
39. Lindop, *Charles Williams*, 168-9, and she had helped him develop his mature verse style, Lindop 226-30.
40. Anne Ridler, *Working for T. S. Eliot* (London: Enitharmon Press, 2000), 5.
41. Anne Ridler, *Memoirs* (Oxford: Perpetua Press, 2004).
42. *The Poems*, II. 179. This the version actually sent to Eliot, from Valerie Eliot's files. Williams gave a variant version to Anne Ridler, which is given in Lindop, *Charles Williams*, 272-3; he establishes that Williams's play was not *Cranmer*.

Eliot responded, also in verse, deprecating his own work and beginning:

> Beware, my boy, the aged maid,
> beware the tongue which is so ven-
> -omous, but be thou not dismayed
> by the austere *paroissienne*!
>
> Her taste in poetry is obs-
> -olete, she gives her benison
> only to sentimental daubs
> of imitation Tennyson.[43]

Their relationship developed further when Eliot started publishing some of Williams's books. His first five novels had been published by Victor Gollancz, but Gollancz had rejected *Descent into Hell*, in an earlier draft, and so had other publishers. In 1937 Williams submitted it to Faber. Eliot did not think the story achieved the momentum 'that kept one turning the pages of *War in Heaven*,' but nevertheless accepted it.[44] Of course, when he came to write the blurb for the jacket he was necessarily more enthusiastic:

> Those who have read Mr. Williams's earlier novels—*War in Heaven, Many Dimensions*, and the others—will not want to be told anything about *Descent into Hell* except that it is one of his best. Those who do not know this author's work will find that when they have read this novel, they will want to read all the others; and when they have read the others, they will wait impatiently for a new one. To them we explain that Mr. Williams is the best living writer of the thriller with a supernatural element. His novels can be read for pure excitement; beyond that, readers will find as much as they are capable of finding. There is also comedy of manners, and acute analysis of human relationships, and finally, exploration of abysses of beauty and horror beyond the borders of the material world. This novel, as the title may suggest, is not recommended reading for hyper-sensitive people alone at night in an empty house.

Descent into Hell also has other debts to Eliot. Glen Cavaliero pointed out that the playwright Peter Stanhope in the book 'is given the status of T. S. Eliot and the consciousness of Charles Williams.'[45] Indeed, Williams occasionally used the name of Stanhope for himself,

---

43. *The Poems*, II. 179. A paroissienne is a female parishioner. The lady apparently preferred Humbert Wolfe; Anne Ridler to Valerie Eliot 24 November 1966, quoted in *Letters* VIII. 719.
44. Lindop, *Charles Williams*, 273; for Eliot's reader's report and further reflections on *Descent into Hell*, see Eliot to Williams 25 February 1937, and notes; *Letters* VIII. 518-9.
45. Glen Cavaliero, *Charles Williams: Poet of Theology* (London: Macmillan, 1983), 80.

imagining himself into the greater fame of his friend. Furthermore, in the novel, the historian Lawrence Wentworth has a recurrent dream of constantly descending a rope. I consider that this was partly suggested by the passage in *Burnt Norton* which begins:

> Descend lower, descend only
> Into the world of perpetual solitude.

Eliot's imagery is based on the layout of Gloucester Road station on the London Underground, where there is both a lift and a spiral staircase.[46] The layout is the same at Williams's local underground station, Belsize Park, so they both had this experience of descent. However, the meaning of the two passages is completely opposed. Eliot has in mind a process of purgation, derived from St. John of the Cross on the dark night of the soul. However, Wentworth is on a progress towards damnation and when he reaches the bottom he is in hell, even though still alive, like the damned in Dante's Ptolomaea.[47] At the opposite end of the scale is Pauline's reaching out to her ancestor, a Protestant martyr at the time of Queen Mary, drawing on the idea of all time being eternally present, as in *Burnt Norton* and *The Family Reunion*.[48] Williams also used this idea in 'Taliessin on the death of Virgil,' in *Taliessin through Logres*, written at around this time. Pauline's final willingness to face her double is recalled by Eliot in Harry's willingness to face and follow the Eumenides in *The Family Reunion*, the play he was working on just after *Descent into Hell* was published.[49] Williams wrote Eliot an enthusiastic letter about *The Family Reunion*[50] and reviewed it positively.[51]

In the later thirties their personal relationship became close, going to plays together and both speaking after a performance of one of Williams's plays.[52] Williams was touched when a mutual friend told him how fond of him Eliot was.[53] He asked Anne Ridler to tell Eliot 'he is the only male love of my life since Nicholson died.'[54] Eliot asked for Williams's *Descent of the*

---

46. *Burnt Norton* III. 25ff., and *The Poems*, I. 917-9.
47. *Inferno* XXXIII, 122-135. See also Eliot, 'Dante,' *Selected Essays* (London: Faber, 1951), 250 (this essay first published 1929), and Williams, *The Figure of Beatrice* (London: Faber, 1943), 141.
48. See note 8 above.
49. *The Family Reunion* Part II, Scene 2, 231-240, 317 and the 'bright angels' at 345. E. Martin Browne recalls hearing Eliot read an early draft in November 1937, *The Making of T. S. Eliot's Plays* (Cambridge: Cambridge University Press, 1969), 90. *Descent into Hell* was published in September 1937.
50. Letter of 30 May 1939, quoted in note to Eliot's letter to Emily Hale, 24 March 1939.
51. *Time and Tide*, 20 (April 8, 1939), 450-1.
52. A performance of Williams's *Seed of Adam* on 9 January 1937; see Eliot, 'Religious drama: mediaeval and modern,' *University of Edinburgh Journal*, 9 (Autumn 1937), *Complete Prose* V. 519-530, note 15; Eliot to Phyllis Potter, 27 October 1936 and notes; *Letters*, VIII. 361-2; Eliot to Emily Hale, 30 December 1936 and 7 and 11 January 1937; Lindop, *Charles Williams*, 265.
53. *To Michal from Serge: Letters from Charles Williams to His Wife, Florence, 1939-1945*, ed. Roma A. King, Jr. (Kent: Kent State University Press, 2002), 32. Michal was Williams's pet name for his wife Florence.
54. Lindop, *Charles Williams*, 301 and see note 38 above.

Dove to review; he wrote privately to Williams saying 'You are, I may say, not only a difficult author, but a difficult author to review,' and describing him in the review as 'this extraordinary eccentric spiritual acrobat,' but praising the book.[55] He echoed Williams's title in the line 'The dove descending' in *Little Gidding*. However, he could make little of Williams's mature Arthurian poetry; *Taliessin through Logres* came out in 1938, but Eliot confessed to others 'I can't understand his poetry' and that it was 'very obscure and I have never cared so much for it.'[56]

Having taken Williams on as a Faber author, Eliot continued to offer him commissions. Eliot asked for a book on the history of magic. This became *Witchcraft*, published in 1941, in which there is little about the serious magic Williams had been involved in—and which Eliot would probably have preferred him to write about—but rather popular magic, *goetia* rather than *magia*, to use Augustine's distinction. Far more important was Williams's study of Dante, *The Figure of Beatrice*, which came out in 1943. They both admired Dante, but Williams took the opposite point of view from Eliot to the doctrines underpinning the *Commedia*. Eliot had said:

> My point is that you cannot afford to *ignore* Dante's philosophical and theological beliefs, or to skip the passages which express them most clearly; but that on the other hand you are not called upon to believe them yourself.[57]

On the other hand, the reaction of Williams on first reading Dante had been, as he later told Dorothy Sayers, to say 'But this is *true*.'[58] In particular he developed his argument that Dante's work was the greatest European example of what he called the Way of Affirmation of Images, for which marriage was 'the clearest possibility.'[59] He contrasted this with the more frequently extolled Way of Negation or Rejection of Images, as expounded for example by monastic writers such as St. John of the Cross, frequently quoted by Eliot.[60] He had already represented these two ways fictionally, in *The Place of the Lion*, in the lives of Anthony Durrant and Damaris Tighe on the one hand, and Mr Richardson on the other. Williams's

---

55. Eliot, 'A Lay Theologian,' *New Statesman and Nation*, 18 (Dec.1939); *Complete Prose*, V. 748-50.
56. Eliot to Theodora Bosanquet 13 October 1941 and to Desmond MacCarthy 14 July 1943, both quoted at note 3 to Eliot's obituary notice of Williams, *The Times*, 17 May 1945, *Complete Prose*, VI. 624.
57. Eliot, 'Dante,' *Selected Essays*, 257.
58. Dorothy L. Sayers, *The Poetry of Search and the Poetry of Statement* (London: Gollancz, 1963), 73.
59. *The Figure of Beatrice*, 15.
60. Williams on St. John of the Cross, *The Descent of the Dove*, 179-81; for Eliot, see the passage quoted as epigraph to *Sweeney Agonistes*, direct quotations from him in *Burnt Norton*, quoted above, and in *East Coker* III. 35-46, review of *The Mystical Doctrine of St. John of the Cross*, *The Criterion*, 13 (July 1934), *Complete Prose* V. 108 and letter to Bonamy Dobrée, 17 April 1936, quoted in *The Poems* I. 945.

concept of the way of affirmation was to have a considerable influence on Eliot, as was his view that the two ways were complementary.

Eliot also commissioned Williams to make a selection of the poems of Wilfrid Gibson, and they discussed two other books: one on the Arthurian legend which Williams died before completing, and one on Wordsworth to be called *The Figure of Power*.[61] The incomplete fragment of the first, *The Figure of Arthur*, appeared after Williams's death;[62] he never started on the Wordsworth book. Eliot also encouraged him to work on the Taliessin poems, but when Williams pointed out that he did not pay him for them, Eliot simply agreed.

In the early years of the war Eliot completed the cycle of *Four Quartets*, giving Williams a signed copy of each one. Barbara Newman has demonstrated that Eliot's quotation of Julian of Norwich at the climax of *Little Gidding* was prompted by Williams's discussion and quotation of her work in his *The Forgiveness of Sins*.[63] In turn, Williams made up for his earlier equivocal response to Eliot's poetry through a review in the form of a dramatic dialogue, a form Eliot had also used.[64] One of his characters praised Eliot as 'one who will have gone, it seems, all his distance,' something he denied to Wordsworth, whom he otherwise greatly admired.[65] However, Williams became indignant when a colleague at OUP said of him, 'Eliot is his great idol.' Williams wrote to his wife that this put him in a 'towering rage' and said: 'Eliot my great idol! I admire him very much; I like him immensely; but my idol!'[66] He also confided to her that he thought that his longer experience of married life might have made him a better poet than Eliot.[67]

Eliot, on the other hand, increasingly admired Williams, frequently praising his work and once beginning a letter to him:

My dear Charles, (unless you are to be addressed as the Blessed Charles, but our Decretarial Etiquette Book contains no guidance for formal approach to the presently Beatified)...[68]

Williams started writing another novel, and this time he went straight to Eliot, who was interested, but advised him:

---

61. Williams, *To Michal from Serge*, 153.
62. In *Arthurian Torso*, see note 1 above. Although Faber had commissioned it, this was eventually published by the Oxford University Press.
63. Barbara Newman, 'Eliot's Affirmative Way: Julian of Norwich, Charles Williams, and Little Gidding,' *Modern Philology*, Vol. 108, No. 3 (February 2011), pp. 427-461; Williams, *The Forgiveness of Sins*, published together with *He Came Down from Heaven* (London: Faber, 1950), 175, 183-5. *Forgiveness* first published 1942.
64. 'A Dialogue on Dramatic Poetry,' *Selected Essays*, 43-58. First published 1928.
65. '*Four Quartets*: A Dialogue on Mr Eliot's Poem,' Williams, *The Celian Moment and Other Essays* (Carterton: The Greystones Press, 2017), 109. First published 1943.
66. *To Michal from Serge*, 75.
67. *To Michal from Serge*, 73.
68. Quoted in a letter by Williams to Joan Wallis, 19 December 1940; Lindop, *Charles Williams*, 359.

what *qua* publisher and blurb-writer I am concerned with, is the slickness of the detective-story-thriller machinery which remains to be built up. That you can accomplish this feat I know; but don't forget its importance in selling the book. And after all, one of your most important functions in life (which I have endeavoured to emulate in *The Family Reunion*) is to instil sound doctrine into people (tinged sometimes with heresy, of course, but the very best heresy) without their knowing it.[69]

This eventually appeared as *All Hallows Eve*, written largely in 1943, which Faber published in 1945. Williams's evocation in it of the London of the dead surely owes something to Eliot's imagined encounter with a ghost after an air raid in *Little Gidding*, published in 1942. And Eliot's passage may in its turn owe something to *Descent into Hell*.[70]

Towards the end of the war Williams had as high a reputation as he ever had, with his poetry being publicly compared to Eliot's.[71] But the weakness of his position in comparison with that of Eliot is apparent from their different responses to a manuscript which was submitted to each of them as publishers. This was the book by Robert Graves which was eventually titled *The White Goddess*. Williams very much wanted to take the book but was unable to persuade his boss, Sir Humphrey Milford, to accept it. He wrote to Graves: 'The Press is not free to do all that it would, nor I even within the Press.'[72] Graves's agent then submitted it to Eliot at Faber, who said it should be published at all costs and was in a position to ensure that this was done. In this, Eliot was again displaying his financial as well as his literary judgement, as the book has never been out of print, and I well remember that in my university days every self-respecting student of literature had a copy of it on their shelves.

Also around this time Williams arranged for Eliot to meet C. S. Lewis, being friends with both of them and wanting them to 'hammer out' their differences over Milton.[73] Lewis and Eliot had already been in touch by letter about Eliot's argument that only poets could judge poetry, which Lewis had rebutted in *A Preface to 'Paradise Lost.'*[74] At their meeting, Eliot said he thought this was Lewis's best book. Lewis took this amiss, not realizing that Eliot would have taken his argument on its merits and not thought the less of Lewis for disagreeing with

---

69. Eliot to Williams, 14 December 1940; Lindop, *Charles Williams*, 377.
70. Medcalf, 'The Dance along the artery—T. S. Eliot and Charles Williams,' 45.
71. *To Michal from Serge*, 173-4, 192.
72. Williams to Graves, 18 July 1944, quoted in Lindop, '*The White Goddess*: Sources, Contexts, Meanings,' in Ian Firla and Grevel Lindop, *Graves and the Goddess: Essays on Robert Graves's 'The White Goddess'* (London: Associated University Presses, 2003), 35-7. See also Lindop, *Charles Williams*, 402-3 and Martin Seymour-Smith, *Robert Graves: His Life and Work* (London: Hutchinson, 1982), 397-8.
73. Lewis to Eliot, 23 February 1943 and 10 March 1943, C. S. Lewis, *Collected Letters* ed. Walter Hooper (London: HarperCollins, 2000-2006), II. 556-7, 561-2 and Charles A. Huttar, 'C. S. Lewis's Appreciation of T. S. Eliot,' in Benjamin G. Lockerd (ed.), *T. S. Eliot and Christian Tradition*, (Maryland: Farleigh Dickinson University Press, 2014), 269.
74. C. S. Lewis, *A Preface to 'Paradise Lost,'* (Oxford: Oxford University Press, 1942).

him. He made a point of not letting literary disagreements interfere with personal friendships; what he objected to was misrepresentation. Williams was apparently just amused.[75]

Williams died in May 1945; Eliot wrote his obituary for *The Times*.[76] He wrote to Humphrey Milford: 'The death of Charles Williams comes indeed as a great shock to me personally. He was a loved friend as well as an author whose work I very much admired and which, I feel, has never yet received its due appreciation.'[77] C. S. Lewis organized a Festschrift in his memory. Eliot intended to contribute an essay on Williams's plays but in the end did not do so.[78] He made amends in other ways: he wrote an essay, 'The Significance of Charles Williams,' for *The Listener* magazine[79] and an introduction to the American edition of *All Hallows Eve*, which is more a memoir of his friendship with Williams than a discussion of that book.[80] He did not collect either of these articles in his own prose collections, nor was the introduction added to the Faber edition of *All Hallows Eve*. Consequently, they are less well known than they should be.

These articles should really be read entire, but I shall take a few points from them. Eliot was impressed both by the man and by his work. Eliot is very complimentary about his personal qualities, saying, for example: 'Williams seemed equally at ease among every sort and condition of men, naturally and unconsciously, without envy or contempt, without subservience or condescension. I have always believed that he would have been equally at ease in every kind of supernatural company; that he would never have been surprised or disconcerted by the intrusion of any visitor from another world, whether kindly or malevolent; and that he would have shown exactly the same natural ease and courtesy, with an exact awareness of how one should behave, to an angel, a demon, a human ghost or an elemental.' He adds 'For him there was no frontier between the material and the spiritual world . . . To him the supernatural was perfectly natural, and the natural was also supernatural.' 'He understood evil because he understood good; he understood evil, not in spite of, but through, his own innocence and purity.' 'With all his radiant benevolence, there were depths to his nature beyond my plumbing. In *Descent into Hell*, for instance, to my mind the most impressive of his novels (all of which fascinate me) there is an understanding of evil and or moral collapse which make me shudder.'[81] 'He seemed to me to approximate, more nearly than any man I

---

75. Roger Lancelyn Green and Walter Hooper, *C. S. Lewis: A Biography*, revised edition (London: HarperCollins, 2002), 283-4. On the general issue see, for example, Eliot, letter to Stephen Spender, 17 November 1933, *Letters* VI, 709-10 and for Spender's own account, *World within World* (London: Faber, 1977 (1951)), 148.
76. 17 May 1945; *Complete Prose* VI. 623-4.
77. Eliot to Humphrey Milford, 16 May 1945, referenced in previous note.
78. Lewis to Eliot, 1 June 1945, 11 and 28 March, 3 and 17 May 1946, *Collected Letters* II. 658, 704, 708-10, and Huttar, *loc. cit.* (Eliot's side of the correspondence is not yet available.)
79. 19 December 1946; *Complete Prose* VI. 772-5.
80. *All Hallows Eve* (New York: Pellegrini and Cudahy, 1948); *Complete Prose* VII. 185-90.
81. For this sentence see note 44 above.

have ever known familiarly, to the saint.' This should be set against Williams's tormented love-life, as documented by Lindop in his biography. About his work, he allows that some of his books were 'frankly potboilers; but he always boiled an honest pot.' He allows that 'very little of his work is quite perfect as literature' but 'he left behind him a considerable number of books which should endure, because there is nothing like them or that could take their place.' 'What he had to say was beyond his resources, and probably beyond the resources of language.' 'What Williams has to give is no mere moral teaching, no mere theory of doctrine. It is a work of imagination, based upon real experience of the supernatural world, of a supernatural world which is just as natural to the author as our everyday world. And he makes our everyday world more exciting, because of the supernatural which he finds always active in it.'

To Emily Hale, Eliot said that Williams, along with a few others, was *une âme pure*.[82] I suspect he knew little or nothing of Williams's relations with his women disciples.

Williams continued to influence Eliot after his death. I have referred to their disagreement about Milton; Williams wrote to his wife 'Even TSE is unsound on Milton.'[83] However, he induced Eliot to rethink his attitude; Williams reported 'a charming letter from TSE . . . saying that I am the only living person to talk intelligently about Milton and the only one to observe what he [*sc.* Eliot] has said—*exactly* what.'[84] In his articles on Williams, Eliot said that Williams's essay on Milton was 'brilliant' and 'quite essential reading.'[85] Eliot repeated his praise in his own second essay on Milton, where he recanted his previous view that Milton had to be a bad influence on poets.[86]

Eliot's next creative work after *Four Quartets* was his 1949 play *The Cocktail Party*. Here we can see Williams's influence on Eliot at full stretch. Suzanne Bray suggested that it 'in many ways resembles a Charles Williams play written by T. S. Eliot.'[87] Eliot uses the same passage from *Prometheus Unbound* that Williams had used in *Descent into Hell*. Eliot's heroine Celia carries the same name that Williams had given to his own second love, Phyllis Jones, and her character may owe something to Chloe in *Many Dimensions*, herself based on Phyllis Jones.

---

82. Letter to Emily Hale, 12 January 1946.
83. *To Michal from Serge*, 27.
84. *To Michal from Serge*, 101. Eliot had previously commissioned Williams to review a book on Milton for his magazine *The Criterion*: E. M. W. Tillyard: *The Miltonic Setting: Past and Present*, *The Criterion* 17 (July) 1938, 738-40 and had said 'I feel more curiosity to know your opinion on this matter than that of anybody else,' Eliot to Williams 29 March 1938, *Letters*, VIII. 858.
85. This essay is the Introduction to *The English Poems of John Milton*, World's Classics edition (Oxford: Oxford University Press), 1940, reprinted in Williams, *The Image of the City and Other Essays* (Oxford: Oxford University Press), 1958.
86. 'Milton II,' *On Poetry and Poets*. C. S. Lewis's *Preface* might also have helped him rethink his view, though he mentions him only briefly.
87. Suzanne Bray, 'Disseminating Glory: Echoes of Charles Williams in the Works of T. S. Eliot,' *Seven: An Anglo-American Literary Review*, Vol. 14, 1997, 62. Most of her article is given to a detailed study of this play. There is also a discussion in Medcalf, 'The Dance along the artery—T. S. Eliot and Charles Williams,' 45-6.

(Williams had also given the name Celia to one of the speakers in his review of *Four Quartets*.) As Williams had done with Phyllis Jones, Eliot here replaced his own lost love, Emily Hale, with an idealized image, as Lyndall Gordon points out.[88] She continues: 'Never did Eliot conceive so lovable a woman, at once assured and sensitive. But then—he kills her in a sensationally cruel way.' When Emily Hale read the script, she of course recognized herself and protested, but Eliot denied that he had used their story.[89] Eliot said that the psychiatrist Reilly was modelled on Heracles in the *Alcestis* of Euripides,[90] and his benedictions are Buddhist,[91] but he seems to me to owe more to the Skeleton in *Thomas Cranmer of Canterbury*, and indeed to Williams's own personality as described by his friends.[92] The play presents both the spiritual quest of Celia, which ends in martyrdom, and the reconciliation and renewal in the marriage of Edward and Lavinia, which result in the conception of their child.[93] These two ways correspond to Williams's Ways of Rejection and of Affirmation of Images; Eliot had previously stressed only the Way of Rejection. Eliot once wrote to Emily Hale: 'I have only proceeded a certain distance along the 'purgative' way, and am yet a stranger to the 'illuminative way': my friend Charles Williams, who died two weeks ago, knew much more about this.'[94] Here, for the first time, he puts into Reilly's mouth the firm statement:

> Neither way is better.
> Both ways are necessary. It is also necessary
> To make a choice between them.
> *(The Cocktail Party, II. 686-8)*

In contrast to both ways is Hell, imagined in very similar terms to the fate of Wentworth in *Descent into Hell*, who cherishes a fantasy woman when the real one proves unattainable:

> Hell is oneself,
> Hell is alone, the other figures in it,
> Merely projections.
> *(The Cocktail Party I. 3. 417-9)*

---

88. *T. S. Eliot: An Imperfect Life*, 415-8.
89. *The Hyacinth Girl*, 310-2.
90. 'Poetry and Drama,' *On Poetry and Poets*, 85.
91. Nevill Coghill in his edition of *The Cocktail Party* (London: Faber, 1974), 222.
92. See especially Hadfield, *Introduction*, and Lois Lang-Sims, *Letters to Lalage* (Kent: Kent State University Press), 1989. Barbara Newman takes the same view, 'Eliot's Affirmative Way,' 440-1.
93. This is only hinted at in the text, but Eliot clearly meant it to be inferred: Eliot to Geoffrey Faber, 29 August 1949, quoted in *The Cocktail Party* ed. Nevill Coghill, 192.
94. Letter to Emily Hale, 28 May 1945.

And when Lavinia says to Peter:

What you've been living on is an image of Celia
Which you made for yourself, to meet your own needs.
(*The Cocktail Party, III. 376-7*)

—Eliot could have used these very words to Williams.[95] Williams could have said the same to Eliot in respect of Emily Hale.

The Cocktail Party marks the high point of Williams's influence on Eliot's work, but similar themes occur in his last two plays, notably the reconciliation of the Mulhammers in *The Confidential Clerk* and the 'certainty of love unchanging' at the end of *The Elder Statesman*.

After the war Eliot, as a publisher, was also able to do something for Williams every writer wants: to keep his books in print, taking them over from their previous publishers where necessary. Under his guidance, Faber & Faber reissued all seven novels in a Standard Edition,[96] with attractive dust jackets; good copies of these editions are now collectors' items. Eliot wrote the jacket copy for them,[97] in which he called them 'supernatural thrillers.' They kept *The Figure of Beatrice* in print and reissued his theological works *The Descent of the Dove, He Came Down from Heaven* and *The Forgiveness of Sins* (the last two in one volume). They did not reprint *Witchcraft*, which Eliot probably regarded as a potboiler, of little permanent interest; it was later reprinted by other publishers. They did not reissue the Arthurian poetry or the plays or collect Williams's numerous articles and essays, as Oxford University Press took care of most of them.

It remains to consider again what they had in common, and what separated them. There is a revealing anecdote which helps to clarify this. In 1943, Eliot and Williams, together with Dorothy Sayers, were invited to help prepare some church services. During a meeting about this—

Williams moved that the phrase 'from the desire of damnation, Good Lord deliver us,' be inserted in the litany. The bishop who was presiding over the meeting pooh-poohed the idea, saying that he could not understand what the phrase could mean.

---

95. Other reminiscences of Williams in *The Cocktail Party* include two from *All Hallows Eve*: Celia's remark that she found in Edward only 'a beetle the size of a man,' I. 2.278 evokes the picture where people look like beetles in Chapter 2; and Lavinia's critical remark about Edward being considerate (as opposed to loving), I. 3. 295-6 is an echo of a similar reflection by Richard in Chapter 5. For further parallels see Grover Smith, *T. S. Eliot's Poetry and Plays: A Study in Sources and Meanings* (London: University of Chicago Press, 1974 (second edition)), 218, 226-7. For a wider discussion see Dominic Manganiello, 'T. S. Eliot, Charles Williams, and Dante's Way of Love,' in *T. S. Eliot and Christian Tradition* (see note 73 above).
96. This was not, however, a critical edition, and there are some misprints.
97. *The Poems*, I, 916.

According to Heath-Stubbs, Williams and Eliot stood up and 'testified that they had both frequently been tempted to desire damnation.' According to Anne Ridler, they merely 'exchanged significant glances.'[98] The scene with the Fourth Tempter in *Murder in the Cathedral* and the spiritual decline of Wentworth in *Descent into Hell* exemplify their understanding of this.

On the other hand they both experienced, or at least imagined, visionary moments: the hyacinth girl passage in *The Waste Land* and the rose garden in *Burnt Norton* and in *The Family Reunion* are examples from Eliot; the movement of the beloved's arm in *Shadows of Ecstasy*, and again in 'The Coming of Palomides' in *Taliessin through Logres*, the vision of butterflies in *The Place of the Lion* and Pauline's meeting with her double in *Descent into Hell* are ones from Williams.[99] In his jacket copy for the novels Eliot wrote of Williams: 'He excels in descriptions of strange experiences such as many people have had once or twice in their lives and have been unable to put into words.' This was also true of Eliot himself.

However, neither was inward-looking at the expense of more public duties. They both strongly emphasized the importance of Christian life in community and were active both in church life and as Christian intellectuals in the wider literary culture. Eliot proposed a Community of Christians who would be a spiritual elite, and the guardians in *The Cocktail Party* exemplify this;[100] the parallel in Williams is the Order of the Coinherence among his friends and 'The Founding of the Company' in *The Region of the Summer Stars*.[101]

As their relationship developed we notice a gradual interchange of roles. I have argued that *The Waste Land* had a profound effect on Williams and led him to reconsider how to write his Arthurian poems, the work which he saw as his most important. So at this time, and as a literary guide, Eliot was dominant. During the thirties, as they got to know each other personally, and Eliot read, in particular, Williams's novels, the influences went both ways. There are more connections between the novels and *Four Quartets* than I have developed here. The two men's friendship became increasingly warm and affectionate. Then, in a way Williams would have appreciated, after his death his influence continued to work on Eliot. What this influence was can be summed up as convincing Eliot of the value of the Affirmative as well as the Negative Way. It may not be going too far to say that that influence from Williams helped Eliot to make his happy second marriage. *Pace* Williams, Eliot may have been the better poet, but Williams became in the end the dominant spiritual influence.

---

98. Lindop, *Charles Williams*, 397-8.
99. *Shadows of Ecstasy* (London: Faber, 1948), 56. First published 1933; *The Place of the Lion* (London: Faber, 1952, 40-4. First published 1931); *Descent into Hell* (London: Faber, 1949), 170-3. First published 1937.
100. Eliot, *The Idea of a Christian Society* (London: Faber, 1939), 42; *The Cocktail Party*, I.2.257, 309 and the end of Act II.
101. Hadfield, *Exploration*, 173-4; Barbara Newman, 'Charles Williams and the Companions of the Co-inherence,' *Spiritus: A Journal of Christian Spirituality*, Volume 9, Number 1, Spring 2009.

ALTERNATIVE HISTORY AND SYMBOLIC GEOGRAPHY IN THE TALIESSIN POEMS

Among the difficulties facing the reader of Williams's Arthurian poems *Taliessin through Logres* and *The Region of the Summer Stars* is that of knowing when and where they are supposed to be set and what their underlying assumptions are. Williams's brief note at the beginning of *The Region of the Summer Stars* is terse to the point of being unhelpful. A good deal is not stated at all, but has to be deduced from the poems, supplied from *The Figure of Arthur* or Williams's other works, or assumed from the historical or literary background. C. S. Lewis, in his generally indispensable commentary,[1] indicates a dauntingly large body of material which he says Williams assumes that you know already. My aim in this paper is to set out and explore these underlying assumptions.

We need to understand that there are several layers of material. Firstly, there is actual history, such as that at one time Britain south of Hadrian's wall was part of the Roman Empire, that the Empire's capital moved from Rome to Constantinople (now Istanbul), that the rise of Islam put it under threat, and so on. Then there is the body of Arthurian literature, which includes stories about Arthur himself and the knights of the Round Table, Lancelot and Guinevere and their illicit love, the quest for the Holy Grail, and Mordred, through whom the Round Table came to an end. There were, as one would expect, variations and differences within this large body of material. Williams made his own additions and refine-

---

1. The second part of Charles Williams and C. S. Lewis, *Arthurian Torso: containing the posthumous fragment of 'The Figure of Arthur' by Charles Williams and a Commentary on the Arthurian poems of Charles Williams by C. S. Lewis* (Oxford: Oxford University Press, 1948).

ments to the stories he inherited, which include the role of Taliessin and his own treatment of places such as Broceliande, Sarras and P'o-l'u.

Then there is the map printed on the endpapers of the original edition of *Taliessin through Logres* and in some but not all reprints, in which a woman's body is superimposed on a map of Europe and the Middle East (see illustration following the Table of Contents). Finally, he embodies in his Arthurian poems several of his key religious ideas, including Co-inherence, Substitution and Exchange, and the role of what he calls the City. I shall not be dealing here with this last body of ideas.[2]

The effect of all this is that Williams has partly inherited and partly created an alternative history and a symbolic geography. Let us start with Williams's own account of what he calls the main theme, as set out in the Preface to *The Region of the Summer Stars*:

> That theme is what was anciently called the Matter of Britain; that is, the reign of King Arthur in Logres and the Achievement of the Grail. Logres is Britain regarded as a province of the Empire with its centre at Byzantium. The time historically is after the conversion of the Empire to Christianity but during the expectation of the Return of Our Lord (the Parousia). The Emperor of the poem, however, is to be regarded rather as operative Providence. On the south-western side of Logres lies the region of Broceliande, in which is Carbonek where the Grail and other Hallows are in the keeping of King Pelles and his daughter Helayne. Beyond the seas of Broceliande is the holy place of Sarras. In the antipodean seas is the opposite and infernal state of P'o-l'u.[3]

The Matter of Britain is the body of medieval literature dealing with the legendary history of Britain. This started with Geoffrey of Monmouth's twelfth century *History of the Kings of Britain*, in Latin, which, despite the title, is a collection of legends with little historical foundation. The Matter of Britain also includes the Arthurian literature, which contains work in many languages written over several centuries.[4]

For Williams, far and away the most important source is Thomas Malory. His book was first printed in 1485 by William Caxton as *Le Morte Darthur*. Williams and his generation read it in the version with modernized spelling by A. W. Pollard, whose 1903 edition was

---

2. There is a good exposition of these, as far as they concern the Taliessin poems, in Glen Cavaliero, *Charles Williams: Poet of Theology* (London: Macmillan Press, 1983), Chapter 5. For a still unsurpassed general account of Williams's thought, see Mary McDermott Shideler, *The Theology of Romantic Love: A Study in the Writings of Charles Williams*, (New York: Harper and Brothers, 1962).
3. Charles Williams, *The Region of the Summer Stars* (London: Oxford University Press, 1950), vii. References are to page numbers as line numbers are not given. First published 1944.
4. An old but still standard introduction is R. S. Loomis, *The Development of Arthurian Romance* (New York: W. W. Norton, 1963). However, Williams did not accept Loomis' contention that the Holy Grail developed from the Celtic cauldron of plenty.

frequently reprinted and was, as C. S. Lewis puts it, at least for their generation, 'the household book.'⁵ In 1934 a manuscript of the work was discovered at Winchester; this had significant discrepancies from the Caxton version which had previously been the only one known. It was edited by Eugène Vinaver with the title *The Works of Thomas Malory* but this was not published until 1947. This was after Williams's death in 1945 and so he had no opportunity to take it into account.

Williams also drew to some extent from earlier sources largely in French, which he knew partly in translation and partly through handbooks, particularly that by J. D Bruce,⁶ and which he summarises in *The Figure of Arthur*. There is nothing to suggest that he read or could read the original old French.

The name Logres comes from Lloegyr, the medieval Welsh name for southern England, excluding Cornwall. Geoffrey has it as Loegria and says it comes from Locrinus, son of Brutus, first king of the Britons and supposedly a descendant of the Trojan Aeneas, founder of Rome.⁷ It refers to that part of Britain which Locrinus inherited. Logres was the version used by the French romances and then by Malory.⁸ Williams, like them, uses it to refer to Arthurian Britain, whose boundaries are not clearly defined.⁹ He might also have been encouraged by the remark of the Arthurian scholar Loomis that Logres 'in Arthurian romance is never far removed from the Other World.'¹⁰

Britain had been a province of the Roman Empire from 43 A.D. until around 410 A. D., the year the emperor Honorius refused its requests for military assistance to enable him to concentrate on fighting the Visigoths, who were already in Italy and threatening Rome. The capital of the Empire had been moved from Rome to Byzantium by the Emperor Constantine in 330 A.D., who renamed it after himself. Williams accepts the change of capital but not its renaming. The Empire had tolerated Christianity since Constantine's Edict of Milan in 313 A.D. and formally adopted Christianity as the state religion in the Edict of Thessalonica of 380 A.D.. The church of the West and the East remained undivided until the schism of 1054 A.D.. The Western and Eastern halves of the Empire had separate subordinate rulers from

---

5. C. S. Lewis, 'The English prose *Morte*,' *Image and Imagination* (Cambridge: Cambridge University Press, 2013), 174. This essay was first published in 1963.
6. *The Evolution of Arthurian Romance from the Beginnings down to the Year 1300* (Baltimore: Johns Hopkins University Press, 1923-4, revised 1928). Williams used the 1928 second edition and cites it in *The Figure of Arthur*, in Williams and Lewis, *Arthurian Torso*, 22 and 34. He also drew on the survey by the occult scholar A. E. Waite, *The Hidden Church of the Holy Graal: its Legends and Symbolism* (London: Rebman, 1909), but he does not cite it.
7. Geoffrey of Monmouth, *History of the Kings of Britain*, edited Michael D. Reeve, translated Neil Wright (Woodbridge: The Boydell Press, 2007), §23, (previously Book 2, Chapter 1), pages 30-1. We do not know which of the several versions of Geoffrey Williams might have read, so I am citing the standard edition.
8. Malory in Caxton's edition also has Logris but Williams uses only Logres. The Vinaver edition has several other spellings.
9. Williams, *The Figure of Arthur*, 53
10. Roger Sherman Loomis, *Celtic Myth and Arthurian Romance* (London: Columbia University Press, 1926), 208.

285 A.D.; the last Emperor to rule over the whole territory was Theodosius I, who died in 395 A.D.. The Western Empire finally fell in 476 A.D.. The Eastern Empire continued on, and kept calling itself Roman, though with gradually shrinking territory, until its final fall to a Muslim army in 1453 A.D.. Williams makes no mention of the division of the Empire and for him it makes more sense to assume that for the poems it did not take place, so that Logres continued to be a province of the undivided Empire. However, Logres was also a kingdom. This made it a client kingdom, in which it had autonomy provided it paid its tribute to the Empire. Judaea under Herod the Great was such a client kingdom and Geoffrey gives Britain a similar status. This, we must assume, was for Williams the status of Logres in his version of the Empire. In Geoffrey and Malory Arthur rebels against paying tribute to Rome, but Williams makes no mention of any tribute.

Byzantium as the original name of the capital, as well as being 'surely one of the most magically resonant place-names in all history,'[11] is easier for verse than Constantinople. In using it for the city Williams was being anachronistic; in this he parallels W. B. Yeats, who used it for his two Byzantium poems. However, Williams says he did this independently and with the intention of developing the figure of the Byzantine Emperor, 'a much more complex image than that of the Roman.'[12] The use of the term Byzantine to refer to the Eastern Empire is also anachronistic; it was introduced by the Renaissance humanist Hieronymus Wolf and had become established by the nineteenth century. Williams uses this also in the poems. We shall return to Williams's creative use of anachronism.

The period after the Roman withdrawal from Britain was known in Williams's day as the Dark Ages, because of the paucity of written records from this period. (Following the work of the historian Peter Brown, it is now generally referred to as Late Antiquity.) In the absence of the Roman armies, Saxon invaders from the continent began to colonize Britain. At some time around the end of the fifth or the beginning of the sixth century there may have been a British leader who campaigned against them and won a reprieve, at least for a period. This was Arthur. The evidence is scanty: it was presented and discussed by E. K. Chambers in a book which Williams probably knew,[13] more briefly by R. G. Collingwood in a book which he certainly knew,[14] and by Williams himself in *The Figure of Arthur*. Collingwood places the crucial battle of Mount Badon, in which Arthur routed his enemies, some time between 493 and 516 A.D. and suggests that there was then peace for forty-four years. Williams quotes the

---

11. John Julius Norwich, *Byzantium: The Early Centuries* (London: Viking, 1988), 35.
12. Charles Williams, *The Image of the City and other Essays* (London: Oxford University Press, 1958), 181. Williams seems to have forgotten that he would have come across this usage frequently in Yeats's *A Vision*, which he first read in its 1925 edition and praised in *Poetry at Present* (Oxford: Clarendon Press, 1930), 58.
13. E. K. Chambers, *Arthur of Britain* (London: Sidgwick and Jackson, 1927) and see below, note 15.
14. R. G Collingwood and J. N. L. Myres (*Roman Britain and the English Settlements*, Oxford: Clarendon Press, 1936), 320-4. Williams refers to this in *The Figure of Arthur*, 8.

tenth century *Annales Cambriae* and puts Mount Badon in 518 A.D. and the last battle, Camlann, in which Mordred was killed and Arthur grievously wounded, in 549 A.D..[15] So the time in which the poems are set is the early sixth century.[16] Williams sums up the possibly historical Arthur in one paragraph[17] and goes on to consider the certainly legendary Arthur of Geoffrey. It was Geoffrey's Arthur who became the Arthur of the Matter of Britain and the possibly historical Arthur dropped out of the picture until historians and archaeologists started wondering whether there might be a historical basis to the stories. For some time, opinion was in favour, but it has now largely moved against this.[18] In any case, for Williams, the Arthur who matters is that of the literary tradition, the Matter of Britain.

Geoffrey's Arthur is an ideal king and almost continuously militarily successful until the last battle. Geoffrey has him successfully conquering most of northern Europe; Malory, particularly in Caxton's version, abridges this account considerably—C. S. Lewis calls it 'the dullest and most incredible part of the whole Arthurian legend.'[19] Williams does not use it at all. Merlin, the knights, the queens, most of the other characters, the round table and the quest for the Holy Grail are not historical and come from the Arthurian literary tradition as it developed from Geoffrey to Malory. Williams does assume a knowledge of this in the poems, but his own account in *The Figure of Arthur* provides this satisfactorily and there is no need to repeat it here. It should be supplemented by his brief notes to *Taliessin through Logres* and the Arthurian material in *The Image of the City*. However, he always reimagines the characters for the roles they play in his own Arthurian world.[20]

He tells us nothing about his choice of Taliessin as the central figure. There was a historical Taliesin (note the spelling), who was a sixth century Welsh poet, some of whose work survives. But over time he became assimilated to a legendary bard who was a shapeshifter. This Taliesin is the subject of the thirteenth century *Tale of Taliesin* which Lady Charlotte Guest included in her translation of the *Mabinogion*.[21] This includes numerous poems upon which Williams draws in 'The Calling of Taliessin.' The line 'And my original country is the

---

15. Williams, *The Figure of Arthur*, 8, which coincides with Chambers, *Arthur of Britain* 15, almost verbatim, though Williams has 'carried' for 'bore,' 'the victors' for 'victorious' and 549 A.D. for 539 A.D. 'Camlaun' in Williams looks like a misprint for 'Camlann.' He retains here the spelling 'Medraut' for Mordred.
16. Williams confirms this in the Author's Note to *The House of the Octopus, Collected Plays* (Oxford: Oxford University Press, 1963), 246.
17. Williams, *The Figure of Arthur*, 10.
18. Ronald Hutton, 'Arthur and the Academics,' in *Witches, Druids and King Arthur* (London: Hambledon Continuum 2006), is a survey by a responsible scholar.
19. 'The English prose *Morte*,' 273.
20. There is a full list of the characters in my 'People and Places in the Taliessin poems: A Register and Gazetteer.'
21. First published 1838–49, but Williams probably used the reprint in Everyman's Library (London: Dent, 1906), which I cite. More recent translations do not include this tale, but there is a modern version, with a discussion, in Patrick K. Ford, *The Mabinogi and other Medieval Welsh Tales* (Berkeley and Los Angeles: University of California Press), 1977.

region of the summer stars,' from which Williams took the title of his second Arthurian volume, comes from here.[22] His role as court poet comes from *Kilhwch and Olwen*, one of the three Arthurian tales in the same collection.[23] This was taken over by Tennyson, who changed the spelling and gave him one line: 'Taliessin is our fullest throat of song.'[24] This would be where Williams first encountered him, and from where he took the spelling.[25] As for his use of Taliessin as the central figure, I suggest that this was influenced by his reading of T. S. Eliot's *The Waste Land*. He was clearly originally baffled by Eliot, as the essay on him in *Poetry at Present* shows. However, I think reading Eliot forced him to reconsider how his own projected Arthurian cycle might work: 'Better be modern than minor' as Keith Mornington says in *War in Heaven*.[26] The blind Greek seer Tiresias plays a part in *The Waste Land*, and Eliot provides a note about this:

> Tiresias, though a mere spectator and not indeed a character, is yet the most important personage in the poem... What Tiresias sees, in fact, is the substance of the poem.[27]

The role of Taliessin in Williams is comparable to this and provides a unifying figure in his cycle as we have it.[28] At one point he said that 'the divine Taliessin himself ... is indeed not so much a man at all as the very Nature of Poetry.'[29] Nevertheless, he intended his next volume, *Jupiter over Carbonek*, to have Percivale in this role instead, saying that 'Taliessin is the poetic imagination in this world and Percivale the imagination of the other end of the universe.'[30]

Returning to the geography we come to Broceliande. Williams would have read about this first in Tennyson, as the forest in which Vivien trapped Merlin.[31] Traditionally it is in Brittany, but Williams relocates it to the North side of the English Channel to make it contiguous with Logres. It is not in Malory, but there is an extensive discussion, complete with a quotation from the original source in the Norman poet Wace, in the notes to Charlotte Guest's

---

22. *The Region of the Summer Stars*, 'The Calling of Taliessin,' 7 and numerous references to the 'summer stars.' The proposal to use the phrase as the title came from C. S. Lewis; see David Llewellyn Dodds (ed.), *Arthurian Poets: Charles Williams* (Woodbridge: Boydell and Brewer, 1991), 6 and note 19.
23. 'Taliesin chief of the bards,' *The Mabinogion*, 101.
24. Tennyson, *Idylls of the King*, 'The Holy Grail,' 300.
25. Chambers, *Arthur of Britain*, also uses this spelling.
26. *War in Heaven* (London: Faber, 1947), 96. First published 1930.
27. T. S. Eliot, *The Waste Land*, note to line 218.
28. I explore Eliot's influence on Williams in more detail in my 'Charles Williams and T. S. Eliot: friends and rivals.'
29. Williams, *To Michal from Serge: Letters from Charles Williams to his Wife, Florence, 1939-1945*, ed. Roma A. King, Jr. (London: Kent State University Press, 2002), 234.
30. Anne Ridler in *The Image of the City*, 174; Williams, *To Michal from Serge*, 156; Williams, '*Taliessin through Logres*: Notes for C. S. Lewis' edited Glen Cavaliero in *Gnomon*, New York, Vol.1, 1965.
31. Tennyson, *Idylls of the King*, 'Merlin and Vivien', 2 and 203.

Mabinogion.³² Williams would also have known it from Chrétien de Troyes' *Yvain*.³³ W. W. Comfort's translation of this, which he would have used, since at the time there was no other, provides a note which runs in part:

> The forest of Broceliande is in Brittany . . . In his version the poet forgets that the sea separates the court at Carduel [possibly Carlisle] from the forest of Broceliande. His readers, however, probably passed over this *lapsus*.³⁴

This may have given Williams the idea that Broceliande could be a sea as well as a forest, as he explained to C. S. Lewis:

> Broceliande is somewhere round Cornwall and Devon, to the west of Logres. It is regarded both as a forest and as a sea—a sea-wood; in this sense it joins the sea of the antipodes which lies among its roots. Carbonek is beyond it; or at least beyond a certain part of it; Carbonek stands between Broceliande and the full open sea, beyond which is Sarras.³⁵

Williams's friend Thelma Shuttleworth called it 'a great wood with deep sea-inlets,'³⁶ which is more rational and half-way between Comfort's note and Williams's for Lewis. As a forest it belongs to the topos or archetypal image of the forest, which occurs so frequently in literature. Williams has an eloquent passage about this in which he notes in passing: 'The forest itself has different names in different tongues: Westermain, Arden, Birnam, Broceliande . . .' and goes on to assimilate it to the sinister dark wood at the beginning of the *Inferno* and, later, to the Earthly Paradise at the top of Dante's Mount Purgatory.³⁷ It is a place of both potentiality and danger:

> but those fewer, now as then, who enter
> come rarely again with brain unravished
> by the power of the place
> ('The Calling of Taliessin', 9)

---

32. *The Mabinogion*, 383ff..
33. He discusses Chrétien and quotes from *Yvain*, *The Figure of Arthur*, 47ff..
34. Chrétien de Troyes, *Arthurian Romances*, translated, with an introduction by W. W. Comfort, (London: Dent (Everyman's Library), 1914), 189 and note on 369.
35. Williams, 'Notes for C. S. Lewis.'
36. [Anne Ridler (ed.),] *The Taliessin Poems of Charles Williams* (Oxford: Charles Williams Society, 1991), 11.
37. Williams, *The Figure of Beatrice* (London: Faber, 1943), 107 and 175. See also *The Figure of Arthur*, 81-2 and Williams's note to *Taliessin through Logres*, note to pp. 3 and 4 ['Taliessin's Return to Logres'].

In Dante, it can lead to Hell or to Heaven. In Williams, as it is also a sea with no boundary, it can lead to their manifestations on earth: P'o-l'u and Sarras.

P'o-l'u, which first appears in 'The Vision of the Empire'[38] in *Taliessin through Logres*, is an addition by Williams to the Arthurian tradition, an infernal state. He calls it 'antipodean Byzantium.'[39] He explained it in prose:

> P'o-Lu [sic] is the Chinese name, of about the period, for the point of Java—the extreme point (nobody knew New Zealand then.)[40]

Williams used the name of a real place, normally spelled P'o-lu, which is the Chinese equivalent of Barus in Northwest Sumatra, not Java. It was a trading centre from at least the tenth century and possibly earlier.[41] For the location, Williams might have been thinking of Dante's Mount Purgatory, also located in the southern seas at a great distance from Europe. But he had a private reason for locating his infernal realm in Java: his second love, Phyllis Jones, married and went with her husband to Java around the time he was working on 'The Vision of the Empire'.[42] Williams does not mention Java in the poems but, in a later poem, after the fall of Logres and the 'bounds of the Empire breaking,' he has the octopods (octopuses) of P'o-l'u advancing, 'feeling along Burma, nearing India.' However, since Broceliande is a sea as well as a wood, its roots are able to grip and so defeat them.[43]

The headless emperor of P'o-l'u is Williams's invention but derives from hostile comments on two Byzantine emperors as reported by the historian Edward Gibbon. The fourth-century emperor Julian, known as the Apostate from his 'noble but ill-fated effort'[44] to restore paganism, was once mocked as 'an ape invested with the purple.'[45] More important was a diatribe against the sixth-century emperor Justinian, best remembered for rebuilding the great church of Hagia Sophia (Holy Wisdom), which is mentioned several times in the

---

38. Williams is inconsistent in his spelling of this placename. After using several variants, he eventually settled on the one here, which I have adopted. There would be a case for normalizing to P'o-lu, but, considering the associations Williams has given it, it is probably better to retain his preferred spelling to retain the distinction.
39. 'The Vision of the Empire' in Charles Williams, *Taliessin through Logres* (London: Oxford University Press, 1938), 12. As with *The Region of the Summer Stars*, references are to page numbers.
40. Williams, 'Notes for C. S. Lewis.'
41. Jane Drakard, *A Malay Frontier: Unity and Duality in a Sumatran Kingdom* (Ithaca: Cornell University Press, 1990), 3-4. I am grateful to Grevel Lindop for this reference.
42. Alice Mary Hadfield, *An Introduction to Charles Williams* (London: Robert Hale, 1959), 146; Grevel Lindop, *Charles Williams: The Third Inkling*, 221 and 248.
43. 'The Prayers of the Pope', *The Region of the Summer Stars*, 59-60.
44. Williams, *The Descent of the Dove* (London: Faber 1950), 50. First published 1939.
45. Edward Gibbon, *The Decline and Fall of the Roman Empire*, ed. H. H. Milman (London: John Murray, 1845), Chapter 22. Gibbon's source is Ammianus Marcellinus, *Res Gestae*, Book 17, Chapter 11.11.

poems. Dante placed him in heaven,[46] but the historian Procopius despised him and suggested, in Gibbon's summary, that 'a monk saw the prince of the dæmons, instead of Justinian, on the throne—the servants who watched beheld a face without features, a body walking without a head &c. &c..'[47] Williams conflated these two comments in his memory when he wrote:

> The Empire is to man, or to some men—lost; the antipodes are the vision reversed, 'the ejection to the creature.' The headless figure is the sight of the Emperor there (the Ape of God); the image is taken from the tale about Justinian. Everything is parodied and holy intellect is lost.[48]

Sarras first appears in Malory as a Saracen (i.e. Arab) city which is converted to Christianity by Joseph of Arimathea. It then becomes a spiritual place.[49] The Holy Grail is finally taken from Carbonek, the Grail castle, to Sarras, from where it is withdrawn into heaven. This is the background to 'The Last Voyage' and to the passages about Sarras (there unnamed) in 'The Prayers of the Pope', 58-60. Malory's sources were the French romances *L'Estoire del Saint Graal* and *La Queste del Saint Graal*, which had not been translated into English in Williams's time, but for which Bruce provided summaries which give more detail than does Malory.[50]

Williams hardly mentions Sarras in *Taliessin through Logres*. However, in *The Region of the Summer Stars* it is introduced as 'the land of the Trinity | which is called Sarras in maps of the soul.'[51] He finally provides a full description of it in the form of a 'deep, strange island' in one of his most splendid passages.[52] We might well ask how it then differs from Byzantium, and indeed Williams says 'Byzantium and Sarras are in a sense one.'[53]

P'o-l'u and Sarras are primarily spiritual states, though imaged as places. The mention of Islam brings us to the principal antagonist to Byzantium as a spiritual power. The expansion of Islam began in the seventh century. By the end of the century the whole of North Africa and much of the Middle East was Muslim and it was a severe threat to what remained of the Eastern Empire. Williams's own summary provides the best background:

---

46. *Paradiso*, Canto VI.
47. Gibbon, *Decline and Fall*, Chapter 40, footnote 18. Gibbon is paraphrasing Procopius, *Secret History*, Chapter 12.
48. Williams, 'Notes for C. S. Lewis.' The quotation is 'The Vision of the Empire,' 10. Wyndham Lewis had used the phrase *The Apes of God* for the title of his 1930 satirical novel.
49. Malory, *Le Morte Darthur*, 13.10; 14.3; 17. 11 and 20-22.
50. Bruce, *The Evolution of Arthurian Romance*, II 308 and 368–9.
51. 'The Calling of Taliessin,' 261–2.
52. *The Region of the Summer Stars*, 'The Founding of the Company,' 98-110.
53. Williams, 'Notes for C. S. Lewis.'

The most opposite earthly frontier of Christendom had been drawn, both in military and metaphysical affairs. Christendom was, and remains, for all its victories, in a state of siege. Byzantium then, like London today [1939], found itself on the edge of war; it almost fell in 717 . . . Locked in a strange debate . . . the two powers contended for the doctrine of the soul. . . No doubt Jew, Mohammedan, and Christian could live comfortably enough together, so long as nothing happened. But the least sneer—and the fires and the massacres might everywhere begin. . . The finished and finite clods of the three Creeds might be untroubled by heavenly sparks; they were prone to be lit by earthly.[54]

Williams makes the rise of Islam contemporary with Logres, another anachronism, and anticipates its eventual victory over Byzantium in the Prelude to *Taliessin through Logres*. However, his main interest is in Islam's denial of the characteristically Christian doctrine of the incarnation:

> the sharp curved line of the Prophet's blade
> that cuts the Obedience from the Obeyed.
> (*Taliessin through Logres*, 'The Coming of Palomides,' 33)

Nevertheless, the Muslim knight Palomides has no difficulty in moving from Ispahan (in present-day Iran) through Muslim Spain and Christian Gaul to Logres, and the failure of his love for Iseult and of his pursuit of the Questing Beast do not seem closely linked to his eventual acceptance of Christianity.

We can now understand 'The Vision of the Empire.' Each stanza, to which Williams has given a Greek letter, celebrates—with one exception—a different province of the Empire. Alpha (α) deals with the capital at Byzantium, Beta (β) with the Caucasian mountain range with its peak at Elburz, Gamma (γ) with Logres itself and Delta (δ) with Gaul, roughly modern France. Williams was thinking of the university of Paris, one of the first in Europe and celebrated for its theological learning: this teaching is summed up in the phrase 'trigonometrical milk of doctrine.' Doctrine is symbolized by the Biblical metaphor of milk;[55] it is trigonometrical both to express the Trinity and also because it is exact knowledge, like mathematics. This is again anachronistic, as the university did not begin operations until the twelfth century. Epsilon (ε) and Zeta (ζ) represent Italy, and, in particular, Rome, the seat of the Pope. Eta (η) is based in Jerusalem and deals with the Fall; following George Herbert's 'The Sacrifice' (lines 201-8),[56] it draws on the legend that the wood of the tree of the knowl-

---

54. Williams, *The Descent of the Dove*, 92-3.
55. I Corinthians 3: 2; Hebrews 5: 12; I Peter 2: 2.
56. This passage is the climactic example in William Empson's *Seven Types of Ambiguity* (Harmondsworth: Penguin, 1961), 232. This was first published 1930 and was widely discussed.

edge of good and evil became that of the cross and sees the Fall and the Atonement as simultaneous. Stanza Theta (θ) presents the opposite of the Empire in the form of the 'antipodean Byzantium' with its headless Emperor. Finally, stanza Iota (ι) shows all the parts of the Empire coming together as do the parts of a body, in an image which is at once classical, Biblical and Shakespearean:[57] 'The organic body sang together.'

To go on to the endpaper map which was printed in *Taliessin through Logres*: Williams thought of it after writing the poems and the designer Lynton Lamb drew it at his direction.[58] This presents the Empire visually as an organic body, that of a woman. Within the Empire her head is Logres, her breasts Paris, her hands cross at Rome, her navel is Byzantium, her womb Jerusalem, her buttocks Caucasia. Outside the Empire is her rectum at Ispahan, the place of rejection because of Islam's rejection of the incarnation. Far in the East is P'o-l'u, which is represented by a tentacle on the edge of the map. 'Sarras, city of the soul, is everywhere by achievement, and so not marked on the map.'[59] The symbolism of the poems moves between geographical and corporeal with a readiness that is startling to those not used to it, and Williams is not averse to a certain harshness in it. I discuss the symbolic geography of the poem further in a separate paper.[60]

Williams's Arthurian world at first seems strange and rather remote. As one reads the poems it gradually becomes more familiar but—and this is a great quality—without losing its strangeness. The assumptions I have laid out fall into place and seem quite natural and one is then free to enjoy the poems and to explore their meaning.

---

57. Aristotle, *Politics* 1253a, Livy 2.32.9; Romans 12: 4–5, I Corinthians 12: 12; *Coriolanus* I. 1. 95ff..
58. Hadfield, *An Introduction to Charles Williams*, 146.
59. Alice Mary Hadfield, *Charles Williams: An Exploration of his Life and Work* (Oxford: Oxford University Press, 1983), 152. The preceding summary of the map is based on her account.
60. 'Metaphysical and Romantic in the Taliessin Poems.'

METAPHYSICAL AND ROMANTIC IN THE TALIESSIN POEMS

*M*y starting point is a comment by C. S. Lewis (*Arthurian Torso*, 197-8) on the way Williams uses imagery of the senses. He says:

On the one hand, it is obviously different from the fully and strictly visual poetry of Milton's 'chequered shade' or Tennyson's 'wrinkled sea'. On the other hand it is equally different from Donne's 'stiff twin compasses' or Mr. Eliot's 'patient etherized upon a table'; it has not that preference for what is harsh and superficially 'unpoetical.' Rather, it has a foot in both worlds. It uses the 'romantic' images in the 'metaphysical' way. The continual quiver of the aroused, yet transcended, senses (like his own 'infinitesimal trembling of the roses') makes the very texture of his writing. It is all 'stuff of Caucasia fashioned in Byzantium' and 'everywhere the light through the great leaves is blown'.[1]

This paper explores some of the ways in which Williams "uses the 'romantic' images in the 'metaphysical' way." This does not have much to do with metaphysics as philosophers understand the term. Two examples of particular relevance to Williams will provide reference points. Since Lewis cites the 'stiff twin compasses,' from Donne's 'A Valediction: forbidding mourning,' this can be one. Williams included it in his 1935 anthology *The New Book of English Verse*. The exact interpretation of the last verse is disputed, a happy precedent for the problems of Williams's own poetry, but the general idea is clear: the beloved, in this case probably Donne's wife Ann, is staying at home and is the fixed foot, whereas the speaker has to travel,

---

1. I have corrected the misprint of Donne's line, which Lewis probably quoted from memory.

but his circle is made accurate by her stability at the centre. Williams might have compared Donne's situation here favourably to that of Dante in the *Vita Nuova*, to whom the God of Love said: 'I am the centre of a circle to which all parts of the circumference are in a similar relation; but you are not so.'[2]

My second example is Marvell's 'The Match.' This is not one of Marvell's best poems, but it has a particular interest for us in that the lady in it is called Celia, which was Williams's pet name for Phyllis Jones, his second love, and which he took from this poem. The idea is that one spark of the explosive stored up in Nature's treasure house can ignite the whole world. Williams used this poem to define what he called 'the Celian moment:' 'the moment which contains, almost equally, the actual and the potential; it is perfect within its own limitations of subject or method, and its perfection relates it to greater things.'[3] This is very close to Joyce's 'epiphany' or to the definition Williams adapted from Coleridge for 'symbol', but I shall come to that later.

Williams included many pages of metaphysical poetry in *The New Book of English Verse*. This was timely, as the reputation of metaphysical poetry was rising rapidly in the 1920s and 1930s, thanks partly to Grierson's 1912 edition of Donne and his anthology of 1921,[4] both of which I imagine Williams might have seen through the press. Grierson's anthology prompted T. S. Eliot's famous review; here Eliot suggested that the metaphysical poets should be seen as part of the normal line of English poetry, that erudition should be incorporated into the poet's sensibility, that the poet should turn his interests into poetry and not 'merely meditate on them poetically,' and that 'the poet must become more and more comprehensive, more allusive, more indirect, in order to force, to dislocate if necessary, language into his meaning,'[5] and that poetry may need to be difficult. This essay practically served as a programme for the poets of the 1930s, and part of my contention is that the Williams of the Taliessin poems is a poet of the 1930s.

On considering the Taliessin poems against the examples I have given, or against Eliot's criteria, they obviously satisfy many of them. There are some passages in which Williams uses conceits in the metaphysical way. One is the comparison between Virgil's search for the right word and Taliessin's for the weak point in the enemy attack in 'Mount Badon' (41-4). Another is the comparison between the sound of a trumpet and a slave girl's arm in 'The Sister of Percivale' (28-30). However, I want to suggest that these passages, though characteristic, are

---

2. *Vita Nuova* XII, as translated by Williams, *The Figure of Beatrice* (London: Faber), 1943, 24.
3. Introduction to *The New Book of English Verse* (London: Victor Gollancz, 1935), 12-13, reprinted in *The Celian Moment and Other Essays*.
4. Herbert J. C Grierson (ed.), *Metaphysical Lyrics and Poems of The Seventeenth Century* (Oxford: Clarendon Press, 1921).
5. T. S. Eliot, 'The Metaphysical Poets,' *Selected Essays* (London: Faber, 1932 rev. 1951), 289.

not perhaps typical of the texture of the poems. I want to indicate an idiom which the following passages demonstrate in increasing degrees of complexity:

> the golden and rose-creamed flesh of the grand Ambiguity
> ('Prelude' to *The Region of the Summer Stars*, 36)

> 'The Wounded Rose runs with blood at Carbonek.'
> ('Taliessin in the Rose-Garden', 51)

> Through the magical sound of the fire-strewn air,
> spirit, burning to sweetness of body,
> exposed in the midst of its bloom the young queen Guinevere.
> ('The Crowning of Arthur', 53-55)

> everywhere the light through the great leaves is blown
> on your substantial flesh, and everywhere your glory frames.
> ('Bors to Elayne: The Fish of Broceliande', 47-8)

> Hued from the livid everlasting stone
> the queen's hewn eyelids bruised my bone;
> my eyes splintered, as our father Adam's when the first
> exorbitant flying nature round creation's flank burst.
> ('Lamorack and the Queen Morgause of Orkney', 1-4)

> O lady, your hand held the bread
> and Christ the City spread in the extensor muscles of your thumbs.
> ('Bors to Elayne: on the King's Coins', 98-9)

> Time's president and precedent, grace ungrieved,
> floating through gold-leaved lime or banked behind beech
> to opaque green, through each membraned and tissued experience
> smites in simultaneity to times variously veined.
> ('The Departure of Merlin', 45–48)

These are all splendid passages, but I ask you also to agree that their meaning floats or hovers somewhere beyond and outside the words. There is not a straightforward comparison between two things, however apparently incongruous, but rather a texture in which the action is interfused with images which carry not only an emotional but a spiritual burden, along with a deliberate elusiveness of meaning. The literal meaning is almost unseizable, so the reader searches for the metaphorical meaning. It is this characteristic, rather than the relatively straightforward use of conceits, which constitutes the main difficulty, which Williams, following Eliot, is happy to court. We can apply to this poetry what Williams said about glory:

> The word glory, to English ears, usually means no more than a kind of mazy bright blur. But the maze should be, though it generally is not, exact, and the brightness should be that of a geometrical pattern.[6]

Williams goes on to say that we should examine the pattern of the glory, and it is possible to paraphrase all these passages. Once we have a grip on the symbolism, we can understand the passages. But the experience of bewilderment followed by clarification is itself part of the meaning of the poetry, and we should be careful not to lose it in turning to the commentaries. I am reminded of two remarks of Eliot in this connection:

> The chief use of the 'meaning' of a poem, in the ordinary sense may be . . .to satisfy one habit of the reader, to keep his mind diverted and quiet, while the poem does its work on him: much as the imaginary burglar is always provided with a bit of nice meat for the house-dog.[7]

> That thrill of excitement from our first reading of a work of creative literature which we do not understand is itself the beginning of understanding.[8]

This interpenetration of the literal with the metaphorical meaning, together with the systematic elusiveness of the literal meaning, makes the texture in these passages of Williams rather different from the seventeenth-century metaphysicals.

Now Williams is not alone among poets of the 1930s in doing this. This we can see by comparing these passages with some by Williams's older and younger poetic contemporaries.

Compare Williams's passage on grace with this:

> O love, the interest itself in thoughtless Heaven,
> Make simpler daily the beating of man's heart; within,
> There in the ring where name and image meet
> (Auden: Prologue to *Look, Stranger!*, 1936, 1-6)

---

6. Williams, *He Came Down from Heaven* (London: Faber), 1950), 33
7. Eliot, *The Use of Poetry and the Use of Criticism* (London: Faber, 1964, first edition 1933), 15.
8. Eliot, 'A Note of Introduction' to David Jones, *In Parenthesis* (New York: Chilmark, 1961.

The elusiveness does not disappear when we learn that the 'ring' is an allusion to the agape or love-feast of the early Christians.[9]

Consider this:

> Before me floats an image, man or shade,
> Shade more than man, more image than a shade;
> For Hades' bobbin bound in mummy-cloth
> May unwind the winding path;
> A mouth that has no moisture and no breath
> Breathless mouths may summon;
> I hail the superhuman;
> I call it death-in-life and life-in-death.
> (Yeats: 'Byzantium,' 9-16, published in *The Winding Stair*, 1933)

The meaning of this briefly is that Yeats will take a walking mummy as his guide to the world of the dead, which is what in this poem Byzantium represents, but the images, though precise, do not have exact referents. The remoteness of this subject matter is comparable to some of Williams's themes. The first two, deliberately convoluted lines, are comparable with this line of Williams:

> The ejection to the creature of the creature's rejection of salvation
> ('The Vision of the Empire,' η, 24)

Understanding either passage is like untying a knot. Now with the very harsh and jagged passage from 'Lamorack and the Queen Morgause of Orkney,' compare this:

> King spider, walks the velvet roof of streams:
> Must bird and fish, must god and beast avoid:
> Dance, like nine angels, on pin-point extremes.
> (Empson: 'Arachne,' 4-6, first collected in *Poems*, 1935)

If you ask 'what kind of spider is a king spider?' or 'what extremes are the angels dancing on?' you will get, you can only get, an answer in terms of paraphraseable meanings along the lines of Empson's own note. Exactly the same is true of the opening of Williams's poem. All these passages share with those of Williams a way of writing which is far more resistant to the ordinary prose understanding than the older metaphysical poetry.

---

9. See John Fuller, *W. H. Auden: A Commentary* (London: Faber, 1998), 146, 149.

To describe this effect we need a different word from elusiveness, which suggests slipperiness, though it is not intended to be derogatory. Nor, though, is this difficulty simply the result of complex allusions making the language obscure. We need a term for the deliberate resistance of some of these passages to ordinary understanding. I find this in a passage of Eliot's poetry:

> Paint me a cavernous waste shore
> Cast in the unstilled Cyclades,
> Paint me the bold anfractuous rocks
> Faced by the snarled and yelping seas.
> ('Sweeney Erect,' 1-4, first collected 1920)

'Anfractuous' is a word Eliot took from Dr Johnson and used to mean contorted, rugged, craggy.[10] You find this anfractuosity in Empson and Yeats as well as in Williams; in all of them there is a deliberate courting of harshness, and in this they all derive from Donne, but Donne is not as harsh in his meaning, as distinct from his diction, as the modern writers.

My last modern example is from a much younger poet:

> In the beginning was the three-pointed star.
> One smile of light across the empty face;
> One bough of bone across the rooting air.
> The substance forked that marrowed the first sun;
> And, burning ciphers on the round of space.
> Heaven and hell mixed as they spun.
> (Dylan Thomas: 'In the beginning,' 1-6, first published in *Eighteen Poems*, 1934)

One commentator takes this to be a rewriting of the opening of Genesis.[11] Although this was written at about the same time as the Taliessin poems and was actually published before them, the processes I have identified in Williams have here gone much further: hardly a phrase has a literal meaning, and the metaphorical references are so many and so dense that you risk losing your way among them.

Williams and the other poets I have cited have taken to heart Eliot's suggestion to see the metaphysicals as part of the main line of poetry—or perhaps Eliot correctly caught the mood

---

10. Eliot, *The Poems* ed. Christopher Ricks and Jim McCue (London: Faber, 2015), I. 500.
11. William York Tindall, *A Reader's Guide to Dylan Thomas* (New York: Syracuse University Press, 1996), 60. First published 1962.

of the moment. However, if Williams and his contemporaries share a quality which is related to the metaphysicals but somewhat different from them, we can ask what it is that makes the difference. There is a larger answer: the whole modern sensibility, and a smaller one, an important part of which is the influence of Hopkins.

Hopkins, although a mid-Victorian, did not have his poems collected until 1918 and Williams himself edited the second edition in 1930. They had a great influence on subsequent poets, including Williams himself. Anne Ridler drew attention to similarities in phrasing and rhythm, and in the use of internal rhymes, between Hopkins and Williams in her Introduction to *The Image of the City*, so I shall not repeat these. Instead, I want to point to Hopkins's ideal which was that a poem should explode,[12] and he sometimes deliberately concocts strange concatenations of words which conceal their meaning until it eventually bursts out from them:

> Only what words
> Wisest my heart breeds dark heaven's baffling ban
> Bars or hell's spell thwarts. This to hoard unheard,
> Heard unheeded, leaves me a lonely began.
> ('To seem the stranger lies my lot, my life', 9-14)
>
> I cast for comfort I can no more get
> By groping round my comfortless, than blind
> Eyes in their dark can day or thirst can find
> Thirst's all-in-all in all a world of wet.
> ('My own heart let me more have pity on,' 5-8)

This kind of writing appealed to Williams's own love of antithesis and paradox, and he also seized on it when he found it in other Victorian poets, for example:

> Nor soul helps flesh more, now, than flesh helps soul.
> (Browning: 'Rabbi Ben Ezra,' 72)[13]
>
> His honour rooted in dishonour stood,
> And faith unfaithful kept him falsely true.

---

12. *The Poems of Gerard Manley Hopkins*, fourth edition, ed. W H. Gardner and N. H. Mackenzie (London: Oxford University Press, 1967), xx.
13. Quoted (slightly incorrectly) in Williams, Introduction to the Second Edition, *Poems of Gerard Manley Hopkins* (London: Oxford University Press, 1930), xi, reprinted in *The Celian Moment and Other Essays*.

(Tennyson: 'Lancelot and Elaine,' 871-2)[14]

There are several parallels to these in Williams. One is the line I quoted earlier from 'The Vision of the Empire.' But his liking for these verbal tangles seemed to grow on him, and there are several more examples in *The Region of the Summer Stars*:

> Flesh knows what spirit knows
> but spirit knows it knows
> ('Taliessin in the Rose Garden,' 164-5)

> the fixing of all fidelity from all infidelity
> ('Taliessin in the Rose Garden,' 190)

> the Rejection of all images before the unimaged,
> the Affirmation of all images before the all-imaged,
> the Rejection affirming, the Affirmation rejecting
> ('The Departure of Dindrane,' 87-9)

> Let the chief of the images touch the Unimaged, and free
> the Love that recovered Itself, nor only an image,
> nor only all the images, but wholly Itself;
> ('The Prayers of the Pope', 171-3)

The following example from Hopkins also introduces a pun:

> Brute beauty and valour and act, oh, air, pride, plume, here
> Buckle!
> ('The Windhover,' 9-10)

William Empson long ago suggested that 'buckle' here carried two contradictory meanings: '*buckle* like a military belt, for the discipline of heroic action, and *buckle* like a bicycle wheel, "make useless, distorted, and incapable of its natural motion".'[15] Now compare with

---

14. C. S. Lewis records Williams's praise of these lines in Williams and Lewis, *Arthurian Torso* (London: Oxford University Press, 1948), 95. Citations from Williams's part of this book are given as *The Figure of Arthur*; those from Lewis's part are given as *Arthurian Torso*.
15. William Empson, *Seven Types of Ambiguity* (Harmondsworth: Penguin, 1961). The first edition appeared in 1930, so Williams could have read this passage. Empson later considered this example 'disagreeable' and apologised for it

that the use of the word 'belted' by Williams in the following passage:

> the sacred stone
> shook with the infinitesimal trembling of the roses
> and melted inwards into the blood of the king
> Pelles, belted by the curse of the Dolorous Blow;
> so rich was the ring and by Merlin royally runed.
> ('Taliessin in the Rose Garden,' 43-7)

'Belted' here means both 'tightly held together' and 'struck', an exact parallel to 'Buckle' in Hopkins.

The most elaborate example of these linguistic tangles is also the finest: Taliessin's memory of having once seen the island of Sarras. This needs a little exposition. The main source[16] was, I suggest, a passage of Dante very important for the imagery of *Paradiso*; in the Primum Mobile Dante sees the nine orders of angels circling round a single brilliant point. Dante's cosmos, with earth at the centre and the heavenly spheres enclosing it, has been turned inside out, with everything depending on and spreading out from the single point of the unmoved mover. The important lines for our purpose are these:

> Non altrimenti il triunfo che lude
> sempre dintorno al punto che mi vinse,
> *parendo inchiuso da quel ch'elli'nchiude,*
> a poco a poco al mio veder si stinse;
> (*Paradiso*, XXX.10-13)

'In like manner, the triumph that sports forever round the point which overcame me *and which seems enclosed by that which it encloses* was extinguished little by little from my sight,' translated J. D. Sinclair.[17]

We also need to be prepared for the theological term 'perichoresis,' referring to the 'co-inherence of the Divine Persons in each other,'[18] which I conjecture Williams took from a

---

in a footnote for the 1947 edition, 226. However, Gardner and Mackenzie cite this ambiguity (without mentioning Empson) as 'the main crux of the poem,' *The Poems of Gerard Manley Hopkins*, 267.
16. There is also an echo of the passage on the 'grace of sense' from Eliot, *Burnt Norton*, II.
17. *The Divine Comedy: Paradiso* translated J. D. Sinclair (London: The Bodley Head, 1946). Williams uses Sinclair's version in *The Figure of Beatrice* and a commendatory paragraph by him is quoted on its dustjacket.
18. Williams, *The Figure of Beatrice*, 92.

then recent theological work which became a standard textbook.[19] Taliessin has had rare moments when everything seemed to work as it should:

> as from a high deck among tossing seas
> beyond Broceliande he had seen afar
> a deep, strange island of granite growth,
> thrice charged with massive light in change,
> clear and golden-cream and rose tinctured,
> each in turn the Holder and the Held—as the eyes
> of the watcher altered and faltered and again saw
> the primal Nature revealed as a law to the creature;
> beyond Carbonek, beyond Broceliande,
> in the land of the Trinity, the land of the perichoresis,
> separateness without separation, reality without rift,
> where the basis is in the image, and the Image in the Gift,
> the Gift is in the Image and the Image in the Basis,
> and Basis and Gift alike in Gift and Basis.
> ('The Founding of the Company,' 97-110)

This verbal energy which Williams seems to have learned from Hopkins, together with the obscurity that can be elusive, or, to use my earlier word, anfractuous, is also characteristic of Williams in his mature work as in that of his younger contemporaries. It represents a break with his earlier smoother style. Here we may compare the comparable break Yeats made with his earlier poetic style, signalled by the poem 'A Coat' in *Responsibilities*, 1914. Yeats made his break twenty years earlier than Williams, but then he was twenty years older.

I suggested that part of the difference between the moderns, including Williams, and the metaphysicals can be accounted for by the influence of Hopkins. Another part which is specific to Williams is due to the influence of the Romantic poets. Here we come to the second part of my subject and also part company with Eliot, for Williams greatly valued the Romantics, and did not share in the depreciation they underwent in the 1930s, for which Eliot was partly responsible. In this, Williams differed from the poets of the 1930s, though significantly, not from Yeats.

Now it is much harder to characterize romantic than metaphysical poetry; it is notoriously one of the most slippery terms in literary or cultural criticism. However, with the

---

19. Williams does not use the term perichoresis here but cites Prestige, who discusses it in detail, G. L. Prestige, *God in Patristic Thought* (London (SPCK, 1952), 291ff. First published 1936. He may have also taken the term co-inherence from this work.

exception of the importance of the imagination, Williams had little sympathy with any of the familiar romantic subjects. Specifically, he had little interest in nature and was very much a man of the city; his interest in religion was in revealed, not natural religion, together with an interest in the possibilities of magic; he urged restraint and control rather than spontaneity; the language of his poems is not the language really used by men, except perhaps by himself, and the elaborate courtesy he practised was as far from the Noble Savage as you could possibly get.

So what did he value in the romantic poets? In his mature years he saw them as it were from the far side of Dante, who for him was the greatest of romantic poets, the teacher of the Way of Affirmation and the theologian of romantic love. Lurking somewhere in the background are also the more visionary passages of the Bible, particularly *Ezekiel* and *Daniel* from the Old Testament and *Revelation* from the New. And remaining from his youth were his occult studies, through which he made contact with a whole tradition of speculative thought, which goes back at least to the mystery religions of the Hellenistic world, and to Neoplatonism, and which also powerfully influenced Blake and Yeats.

Starting with Dante, then, since Williams's whole cast of mind was not so much influenced as determined by Dante, the Taliessin poems can to a considerable extent be glossed with passages from *The Figure of Beatrice*. The epigraph to *Taliessin through Logres* is taken from Dante's *Monarchia*, and it reads, in Williams's own translation: 'The proper operation (working or function) is not in existence for the sake of the being, but the being for the sake of the operation.'[20] Williams considers this 'great sentence' a 'governing clause in all his [sc. Dante's] thought,' and in the Taliessin poems it accounts, for example, for his treatment of Arthur and of Guinevere. But here I am specifically concerned not with thought but with imagery, and I want to pick out two points in Dante which are of interest because Williams incorporated them into his symbolic geography.

In discussing the opening of the *Commedia* Williams considers the image—we might call it a topos or an archetype—of a wood, giving numerous examples from literature and mythology, so many in fact, that 'the whole earth seems to become this one enormous forest, and our longest and most stable civilizations are only clearings in the midst of it'.[21] One of these forests is Broceliande, the forest of Arthurian legend in the Taliessin poems,[22] and also of Dante. At the opening of the *Commedia* Dante is in one version of it, the dark wood, and after going through Hell and climbing the mountain of Purgatory he finds himself in a very

---

20. *The Figure of Beatrice*, 40. There is also a looser translation in *The Descent of the Dove* (London: Faber, 1950), 132. First published 1939.
21. *ibid.* 107.
22. Williams, *The Figure of Arthur*, 81-2.

different one, that of the Earthly Paradise.[23] This second forest, described in Canto XXVIII of the *Purgatorio*, may have contributed to the beautiful description of Broceliande in 'The Departure of Merlin':

> there no strife
> is except growth from the roots, nor reaction but repose;
> vigours of joy drive up; rich-ringed moments
> thick in their trunks thrive, young-leaved their voices
> ('The Departure of Merlin,' 22-4)

The other specific image Williams took from Dante is the Third Heaven. In the *Paradiso*, the blessed appear to Dante in the successive spheres or heavens of Ptolemaic astronomy. The third heaven is the heaven of Venus, the goddess of love, and is therefore where Dante meets redeemed lovers. Williams discusses this twice,[24] and is particularly struck by the fact that the shadow of earth was thought to extend in a cone as far as the planet Venus.[25] In the symbolic geography of the Taliessin poems the Third Heaven is, according to Williams's gloss, 'that of accomplished states of being, and is as far as human understanding can go.'[26] The fullest description is this:

> The cone's shadow of earth fell into space,
> and into (other than space) the third heaven.
> In the third heaven are the living unriven truths,
> climax tranquil in Venus. Merlin and Brisen
> heard, as in faint bee-like humming
> round the cone's point, the feeling intellect hasten
> to fasten on the earth's image; in the third heaven
> the stones of the waste glimmered like summer stars.
> ('The Calling of Taliessin,' 250-257)

The passage brings us back to English romantic poetry with the reference to 'the feeling intellect.' This is from Wordsworth, who turns up twice in the Taliessin poems, charmingly

---

23. Another version is the wood of the suicides in *Inferno* XIII, mentioned by Williams in 'The Calling of Taliessin,' 144, but this is not material to my argument.
24. *The Figure of Beatrice*, 58, 202.
25. *Paradiso* IX.118-9.
26. [Anne Ridler, ed.], *Notes on The Taliessin Poems of Charles Williams* (Oxford: Charles Williams Society, 1991). This includes Williams's own notes as well as those by others.

and anachronistically, as a 'northern poet.'[27] Williams's other mention of 'feeling intellect' is also in a context where the third heaven is invoked. Merlin, he tells us:

> sent his hearing into the third sphere
> once by a northern poet beyond Snowdon
> seen at the rising of the moon, the *mens sensitiva*,
> the feeling intellect, the prime and vital principle,
> the pattern in heaven of Nimue, time's mother on earth,
> Broceliande.
> ('The Son of Lancelot,' 52-7)

We know from *The Figure of Beatrice* that Williams considered Wordsworth's *Prelude* the nearest thing in English to the way of affirmation as set out by Dante in the *Commedia*, and the 'feeling intellect' is, I suggest, his equivalent from Wordsworth for what he takes Dante to mean by the third heaven. Near the beginning of *The Figure of Beatrice* he quotes the same passage from the *Prelude* as that referred to here, which extols the feeling intellect.[28] However, the passage which actually defines it comes a little earlier in the poem and does not use this phrase:

> There I beheld the emblem of a mind
> That feeds upon infinity, that broods
> Over the dark abyss, intent to hear
> Its voices issuing forth to silent light
> In one continuous stream; a mind sustained
> By recognitions of transcendent power,
> In sense conducting to ideal form,
> In soul of more than mortal privilege.
> (Wordsworth: *The Prelude* (1850), XIV, 63-77)

Now this suggests the world-soul of the Neoplatonists or the *Anima Mundi* of Yeats. Williams does not follow out this implication, but instead, as it were baptizes Wordsworth's conception. There are two stages to this process: firstly, he associates Wordsworth's feeling intellect with Dante's third heaven. And then, mentioning the third heaven on its own, without mentioning any other heaven, would immediately recall to any Christian the words

---

27. 'The Son of Lancelot', 53; 'The Coming of Galahad', 54.
28. Wordsworth, *The Prelude* (1850 text), XIV. 206-227. Williams habitually read *The Prelude* in Wordsworth's final text of 1850, not the 1805 text which has largely replaced it.

of St Paul: 'I knew a man in Christ above fourteen years ago, (whether in the body, I cannot tell; or whether out of the body, I cannot tell: God knoweth;) such a one caught up to the third heaven.'[29]

Wordsworth therefore provides a kind of English equivalent to Dante, and they both contribute not only some of the governing ideas but also some of the details of Williams's symbolic system. Another such contribution of Wordsworth is the dream of the Bedouin carrying the stone and shell to save them from an approaching flood, in Book V of *The Prelude*. The shell and the stone are, for Wordsworth, poetry and mathematics, but in Williams they become polar opposites, which can be set out in a table:[30]

Shell	*Stone*
Poetry	Mathematics
Vital	Geometric
Broceliande	Byzantium
Nimue	Third Heaven
Uncut hazel	Cut hazel
Feeling	Understanding
Sound	Measurement
Beauty of romantic states	Exploration of romantic states

The following passage illustrates this polarity and also takes up Wordsworth's image of the approaching and devouring sea:

> 'My lords and fathers the Druids between the hazels
> touched poems in chords; they made tell
> of everywhere a double dance of a stone and a shell,
> and the glittering sterile smile of the sea that pursues.'
> ('The Coming of Galahad,' 49-52)

Ultimately, of course, as with all polarities, the opposites have to be united, or as Williams put it: 'the shell has to be fitted to the stone.' This is summed up in the figure of Galahad, and in the following passage:

> The moon of irony shone on Lancelot at Carbonek,
> the moon of defeated irony on Blanchefleur at Almesbury;

---

29. II Corinthians 12: 2.
30. See Lewis, *Arthurian Torso*, 168, and *Notes on the Taliessin Poems*, 65.

her hands and head were the shell bursting from the stone
after it has bred in the stone; she was bright with the moon's light
when truth sped from the taunt; well she nurtured Galahad.
('The Coming of Galahad,' 157-161)

These passages begin to show how Williams's poetic imagination worked in taking up symbols, transforming them, and integrating them into a symbolic system of his own. And what he valued most in the romantic poets seems to have been these visionary aspects. However, the desire to create a symbolic system of imagery is one respect in which Williams differs both from the metaphysicals and from most of the romantics. The metaphysicals did not take over or invent a symbolic system; they took their imagery from romantic love, the Christian faith, and their surroundings. The romantics had favourite themes, but in general they were not systematic and would not have wanted to be.

There is an exception to this: Blake, particularly in his later and longer poems which became known as the Prophetic Books. Williams was greatly impressed by the last of these, *Jerusalem*, which he discusses several times, though always with strong reservations.[31] For my purpose the most relevant discussion is in the seventh chapter of *The Forgiveness of Sins*, where he gives the following account of it:

> This poem, like the other Prophetic Books, is concerned with the loves and wars, the destruction and salvation of great super-human beings. These beings pass from one kind of existence to another; from a world of life to a world of death, and again to a world of life. It is true we cannot be very much interested in those great forms themselves; they are not sufficiently clear for us to know or distinguish them, except after very careful study. But this is not so much incompetence on Blake's part as one might unwisely suppose. What he thought mattered was not 'individuals' but 'states'; it was these states of being which he desired to define and declare, and individuals in his verse—even his own giant individuals—are only there to reveal the states of being in which they exist.[32]

Although he goes on to say 'Poetically, this was no doubt a fault or at least a misfortune,' the concentration on superhuman individuals and states can to some extent be applied to the Taliessin poems, and Williams's Palomides does indeed pass from a world of life to a world of death and again to a world of life. Williams's concept of Logres also derives from Blake's of Albion, as is clear from this note of his:

---

31. *The English Poetic Mind* (Oxford: Clarendon Press, 1932), 185-7, the 1941 essay 'Blake and Wordsworth' in *The Image of the City* (London: Oxford University Press, 1958) and the discussion in *The Forgiveness of Sins* cited next.
32. Williams, *The Forgiveness of Sins*, in *He Came Down from Heaven*, 177.

> The figure called Albion in Jerusalem is said ... to be a symbol of 'the true relation of Time and Space with Eternity', and so on; and this is no doubt true. But it is also true that the name stands, as it always has, for England ... England itself is summoned to be a true relation of Time and Space with Eternity.[33]

The whole concept of the symbolic geography in the Taliessin poems derives from Blake. Long ago John Heath-Stubbs suggested that that there was 'an almost exact correspondence between Sarras and Eden, Broceliande and Beulah, Albion and Logres, and P'o-l'u and Ulro.'[34] Now Blake and Williams were both drawing on occult tradition, but Williams here has a number of distinctive features.

Williams superimposed a woman's body on the map printed on the end-papers of the original edition of *Taliessin through Logres*, and the symbolism of the poems moves between geographical and corporeal with a readiness that is startling to those not used to it. He expounds it in 'The Vision of the Empire,' where we again find the unseizable aspect of the imagery and note that Williams is not averse to a certain harshness in it. Even more important is the governing idea of this poem: 'The organic body sang together.' The concept of a state as a body corporate goes back to Aristotle.[35] St Paul argues from the care that the members should have of one another that the same should be true of members of the body of Christ, i.e. the church, stating that:

> those members of the body, which we think to be less honourable, upon these we bestow more abundant honour; and our uncomely parts have more abundant comeliness.[36]

This, I am sure, would have been Williams's justification of his treatment of Caucasia in the poems.

The actual places mentioned in the poems, and so the candidates for this symbolic geography, fall into three groups, though the divisions between them are not sharp. Firstly, there are simple place or geographical names with little or no special symbolic significance, such as the Thames, Wales, Athens, Lombardy, Jura. Then there is a group of places which carry both a literal and a symbolic meaning, such as Byzantium, Gaul, Caucasia or Cordova. Some of them have a significance in terms of the organic body given on the map; examples are Caucasia, Gaul and Jerusalem; and some do not; examples of these would be Apennine, Cappadocia or the Thebaid. Thirdly, there is a group of places which have virtually no physical location at

---

33. *ibid.* 180. Cf. also *The Figure of Arthur*, 80.
34. Heath-Stubbs, John: 'Charles Williams,' *The Literary Essays* (Manchester: Carcanet), 1998), 161. This essay was first published separately in 1955.
35. Aristotle, *Politics* 1253a.
36. I Corinthians 12: 23.

all, such as Sarras and of course the Third Heaven. But there are also some places which hover or tremble between the second and the third group: Logres is not just Arthurian Britain but an imagined political state which represents an ideal community; Broceliande is not only a physical territory, which includes both forest and sea, but also a spiritual state; and the mysterious London-in-Logres is the capital of Britain as Logres, and so by implication Camelot. Fortunately, Williams confirms this for us once,[37] but the phrase, which he uses several times, gives us the sense of our ordinary capital city strangely transformed into a manifestation of Arthurian Britain, of the City in Williams's special sense. And there are also places which Williams happens not to have made much of, but which he might have done, such as Verulam, Canterbury, or Monsalvat.

The result of this is, on the large scale, rather similar to the use of imagery on the smaller scale which I started with. I called it elusive then, or sometimes anfractuous, but we can now be a little more precise, and say that the extent to which the language is literal or symbolic is itself constantly changing, rather like the varying perspectives in a Cézanne or cubist painting. The reader is to be aware of the actual and potential associations of the place names,[38] whose significance is not literal but has a varying symbolic weight in passages such as these:

> The wonder that snapped once in the hollow of Jerusalem
> was retrieved now along the level of the bulwark
> to where the hands of Galahad were reeved on the prow:
> the hollow of Jerusalem was within the hollow of his shoulders,
> the ban and blessing of the empire ran in his arms
> ('The Last Voyage,' 63-66)
>
> an image springing from a tangle of ringing names—
> Thames, Camelot, Carbonek, Pelles and Arthur,
> Logres, Wye, Helayne, Broceliande,
> Byzantium, the Empire...
> ('The Calling of Taliessin,' 237-40)

Having dealt with the symbolic geography in some detail, this is the place to consider the characters in the story. Williams's approach contrasts with that of Blake, whose characters he thought it impossible to be interested in.[39] They are not simply the characters of the

---

37. 'Taliessin in the School of the Poets,' 1.
38. Cf. Lewis's discussion of Milton's use of proper names in *A Preface to 'Paradise Lost'* (London: Oxford University Press, 1942), 40-1. This book was dedicated to Williams.
39. 'But the people—the personages, rather—it is they in whom it is impossible to be interested,' *The English Poetic Mind*, 185.

Arthurian legends imagined against a period setting, in the way Tennyson or Swinburne imagined their Arthurian poems. Nor are they personified abstractions, like the characters in *Pilgrim's Progress*. Instead, they are symbolic personages,[40] like most of the characters in the *Divine Comedy*. Both Dante's characters and Williams's represent qualities in the soul, as well as being individuals in whom we can be interested. In his own words: 'The knights are capacities of man and modes of being (but also knights).'[41] Of course I am not suggesting that Williams approaches Dante in stature as a poet; I am referring to an aspect of technique. And we notice with his characters something similar to what we noticed with the geography: some of them carry a symbolic meaning we can learn, but they do so to a varying extent, from unnamed slaves and pirates, through the principal roles who are indeed mostly knights, to elusive creations such as Merlin, Nimue, Brisen and the Emperor at Byzantium. And the extent to which they carry this symbolic burden is itself unpredictable and changing, and this partly accounts for the persistent feeling of strangeness that is a real and definite quality in the poems.

Williams's systematic use of symbolism has emerged from considering his debt to the romantics, so we can now consider the third of the original romantic poets, Coleridge. His importance to Williams seems to be not in his own practice of visionary poetry but in his discussion of poetic symbolism in *The Statesman's Manual*.[42] Williams develops this in his discussion of the image, a word he prefers to symbol, in two ways, which he develops in connection with the image of Beatrice in Dante. 'First,' he says, 'the subjective recollection [of Beatrice] within him [Dante] was of something objectively outside him; it was an image of an exterior fact and not of an interior desire. It was sight and not invention. Secondly, the outer exterior shape was understood to be an image of things beyond itself.' He then goes on to paraphrase Coleridge: Coleridge, he says, 'said that a symbol must have three characteristics:

1. it must exist in itself,
2. it must derive from something greater than itself,
3. it must represent in itself that greatness from which it derives.'

Now this definition is more far-reaching than it may first appear. The criterion of objectivity would not have been satisfied by Coleridge's symbols in his poetry and would only have been partially satisfied by Wordsworth. The visionary poetry of the romantics is at least as

---
40. I take these terms from the Introduction to the translation of *Hell* by Dorothy L. Sayers, Dante: *The Divine Comedy: Hell* (Hamondsworth: Penguin, 1949), 12-16. Sayers dedicated her translation to the memory of Williams and frequently wrote of her debt to him. See also her *Introductory Papers on Dante* (London: Methuen, 1954), 6-7.
41. Williams, *The Image of the City*, 176.
42. *The Statesman's Manual*, 1816, 36-7; cited from John Beer, *Coleridge the Visionary* (London: Chatto, 1959), 138; also in Coleridge, *Collected Works*, Vol VI, *Lay Sermons* (Princeton: Princeton University Press, 1972), 30.

much an expression of interior states as it is of anything objective. Williams was attempting something different. Equally important is the criterion of continuity between the symbol or image and that which it represents. This is radically different from the moderns, at least those since Yeats. Eliot wrote of the 'dissociation of sensibility' and the need for a poet to find an 'objective correlative' which will link the emotion and the object.[43] This implies a discontinuity which a symbol can bridge. Younger poets took this up using Marxist and Freudian ideas of the discontinuity between economic base and ideological superstructure or between manifest and latent meanings.

I earlier considered ways in which Williams resembled his contemporaries. But it is important to realize here his difference from them, which arises from his poetics, which have quite different sources and aims. Firstly, he wanted to write some kind of narrative, and to use the Arthurian legends as his material. Secondly, he wanted to have characters whom one could be interested in, unlike Blake's, and more like those of Yeats, whom he praised for giving English verse a new mythology.[44] And, thirdly, he wanted this material to carry the sense of spiritual states and struggles of which he was so aware, and which he explored in his critical and theological work. He did not want simply to meditate on the Arthurian legends poetically, in Eliot's phrase, but to use them to convey spiritual states best expressed in mythological terms. And in this he also admired Yeats, whom he praised for 'the continual suggestion of other possibilities than the normal mind is conscious of.'[45]

Now there are two ways of using symbolism to represent the immaterial, and, conveniently for us, the classical discussion of them in English is by C. S. Lewis, in a book Williams admired, *The Allegory of Love*, published in 1936.[46]

> On the one hand you can start with an immaterial fact, such as the passions you actually experience, and can then invent visibilia to express them . . . this is allegory . . . . But there is another way of using the equivalence, which is almost the opposite of allegory, and which I would call sacramentalism or symbolism. If our passions, being immaterial, can be copied by material inventions, then it is possible that our material world in its turn is the copy of an invisible world. . . . The attempt to read that something else through its sensible imitations, to see the archetype in the copy, is what I mean by symbolism or sacramentalism . . . The difference between the two can hardly be exaggerated. The allegorist leaves the given—his own passions—to talk of that

---

43. *Selected Essays*, 288, 145.
44. *Poetry at Present* (Oxford: Clarendon Press, 1930), 68.
45. *ibid.*, 63.
46. Williams's letter of praise, in reply to one of Lewis praising *The Place of the Lion*, is quoted in Roger Lancelyn Green and Walter Hooper: *C. S. Lewis: a biography* (London: HarperCollins, 1974 revised 2000), 137. It led to their friendship. Williams frequently cited and praised this work.

which is confessedly less real, which is a fiction. The symbolist leaves the given to find that which is more real.[47]

Lewis also touches on the affinity of sacramentalism or symbolism with the Hermetic or Neoplatonic tradition, which in its later forms becomes the occult tradition which lies behind Blake, Yeats and Williams. But what is important here is the hard antithesis between the two types of symbolism, allegorical or sacramental, even though Lewis also says that the two things are 'closely intertwined.' This kind of hard antithesis is characteristic of Lewis's thought;[48] Graham Hough noted the strong emotional colouring of this passage and analyzed the distinction as that between 'a mere rhetorical device as against a whole mode of apprehension,'[49] while Northrop Frye pointed out the possibility of a 'sliding scale' in which symbols bear a varying rather than a fixed relationship towards the reality they represent.[50] Frye instances the metaphysical conceit, the French symbolist inexplicit suggestiveness and the Eliotic objective correlative as examples of the different kinds of relationship between art and nature, whether continuous or discontinuous.

Now let us turn to Williams and ask whether his use of symbolism is allegorical or sacramental. Here I think we find a sliding scale of the kind Frye mentioned. At one end are symbols that are almost wholly allegorical: the cut hazel represents order, measurement and power, and the uncut hazel represents the actuality of grace.[51] Once you have learned this, you can see it as appropriate, but you would not have guessed it, and the symbol is at some distance from what it represents. Similarly, though Williams does not tell us, the colours of gold, rose and cream, particularly in combination, represent the divine.

Further along the scale is the use of symbolic animals. Many of these are simply emblematic: the stooped horse, the king's falcons, the seamews, the centaurs and so on. Williams's use of these seems to me mainly emblematic, as in the Psalms, where the bull, lion, and dog stand for particular qualities, but are not asked to carry a heavier symbolic burden. But some have a greater life: the unicorn, which represents Taliessin's vocation, the fish of Broceliande which represents 'the strange quality in romantic love,'[52] and the two wolves in 'The Son of Lancelot': the grey wolf who is Lancelot, and the white wolf, who is Merlin. Let us examine one in more detail: this is the questing beast that appears to Palomides when he looks too

---

47. C. S. Lewis, *The Allegory of Love* (London: Oxford University Press, 1936), 44-5.
48. Stephen Medcalf points how Williams emphasized co-inherence where Lewis emphasized division, 'Objections to Charles Williams,' 210, in Brian Horne (ed.): *Charles Williams: A Celebration* (Leominster: Gracewing, 1995).
49. Graham Hough, *A Preface to The Faerie Queene*, London: Duckworth, 1962), 100ff..
50. Northrop Frye, *Anatomy of Criticism* (Princeton: Princeton University Press, 1957) 91-2.
51. *The Image of the City*, 179 and 182.
52. *Notes on the Taliessin Poems*, 31.

long at Iseult:

> I heard the squeak of the questing beast,
> where it scratched itself in the blank between
> the queen's substance and the queen.
> ('The Coming of Palomides,' 130-3)

Williams makes Palomides's endless futile quest for this beast, a standard theme in Arthurian writing, embody his obsessive and futile passion for Iseult. Now compare this with another poet's treatment of the same situation:

> O Love, be fed with apples while you may,
> And feel the sun and go in royal array,
> A smiling innocent on the heavenly causeway,
>
> Though in what listening horror for the cry
> That soars in outer blackness dismally,
> The dumb blind beast, the paranoiac fury.
> (Robert Graves: 'Sick Love,' 1-6, published 1929)

This 'dumb blind beast' represents the obsessive passion of the lover as does Williams's questing beast, but it has no life outside Graves's poem: Williams, however, has chosen a mythology in which the beast has an objective existence, which Palomides gives too much of his life to pursuing. It exists in itself, and is sight and not invention, whereas Graves's beast is a rhetorical device. Williams has chosen this idiom because he believes that what we call feelings can be modes of apprehension, benign, as with the fish of Broceliande, or demonic, as here.

Still further along the scale is the imagery from mathematics: the 'trigonometrical milk of doctrine' in the breasts of Gaul, the line of the body in 'Taliessin in the School of the Poets', or the 'diagram of desire' which pervades 'The Coming of Palomides.' Take one particular example:

> Proportion of circle to diameter, and the near asymptote
> Blanchefleur's smile; there in the throat her greeting
> sprang, and sang in the one note the infinite decimal.
> ('The Sister of Percivale,' 61-3)

Blanchefleur's smile, like that of Beatrice in the *Paradiso*, has an infinite quality to it,[53] which is compared to two mathematical ideas which also have an infinite aspect: the proportion of circle to diameter is the number π, which is an infinite decimal which never recurs;[54] an asymptote is a line which approaches another line increasingly closely but meets it only at infinity. Both use infinity to define something exact, which is part of the point. On its own, we have a double metaphysical conceit, in which the symbols are illustrative or allegorical, but in the context of the Taliessin cycle, the mathematical images link up with those elsewhere, and move from being conceits to become modes of apprehension. In particular they reveal how Williams perceived the human body. We remember his remark on the body 'of which the centre line is given, obviously, and yet never quite given.'[55]

The result is that the extent to which the images are allegorical, on the one hand, or sacramental, on the other, the place where they stand on the sliding scale, is neither consistent nor constant; they vary, according to the type of image, the particular use, and also according to how well the reader knows or remembers the poems. And since images used allegorically are rhetorical devices, whereas those used sacramentally are modes of apprehension, the result is that our capacity for apprehending spiritual states is being constantly aroused and satisfied, with a constant play of awareness around the edges of our vision. In considering the symbolic geography, I compared Williams's usage to that of Cézanne or a cubist painting: different degrees of symbolism are used for different purposes. But for his general use of imagery, with this varying degree of suggestiveness, I would vary the metaphor and suggest the constantly varying sparkle and glitter you see in the mosaics of the Byzantine school in Ravenna and Venice, which vary according to the light and the position of the viewer as well as according to the composition and the setting of the individual tesserae.

And this is my conclusion on how Williams uses romantic symbols in a metaphysical way. In a way it returns us to the original meaning of metaphysical, rather than its specialized sense in literary criticism: Williams's poetic technique, and his use of mythology and symbolism are all directed to the end of evoking states of being which most of us have only a fleeting awareness of, but which also obstinately persist and seem to underlie ordinary experiences. When he is successful—or perhaps I should say, when we are receptive to his work—Williams achieves what he praised in Yeats: 'the continual suggestion of other possibilities than the normal mind is conscious of.' It is of the essence of it that the degree to which the

---

53. 'The kind of life which it [*sc.* the image of Beatrice] involves is capable of infinite growth,' *The Figure of Beatrice*, 190.
54. Both Alice Mary Hadfield, *Notes on the Taliessin poems*, 54, and Roma King, *The Pattern in the Web: The Mythical Poetry of Charles Williams* (Kent: Kent State University Press, 1990), 83, seem to think π recurs, but it is not only irrational, i.e., inexpressible as a ratio, which would indeed give a recurring decimal, but transcendental, i.e. inexpressible in an algebraic equation, and so does not recur.
55. *Notes on the Taliessin Poems*, 35.

images are allegorical or sacramental is not fixed; spiritual states cannot be evoked through flat symbolism: there has to be some indirection, some elusiveness, to achieve the shimmering effect and the suggestiveness we value.

There are other aspects of this which would be worth exploring. But I want to end with a reference to Yeats, who has turned up quite frequently in this paper. Williams really is very like Yeats: the preoccupation with mythical and legendary material, coupled with a tendency to mythologize his own immediate circle; the derivation from the romantic poets; the interest in occult traditions founded on practical experience; the systematic symbolism, and the desire for a highly polished surface, though in Yeats it is burnished, whereas in Williams it glitters. Of course Yeats is the greater poet, in the range and depth of his gifts and output, and in the consistent quality of his workmanship, but Williams is the same kind of poet, and if we want to see him in a literary tradition it is with Yeats that he belongs.

TWO BOOKS ON THE HOLY GRAIL

The Holy Grail has become such a trap for the unwary that a new book that is clear, comprehensive, and above all sane, is greatly to be welcomed. This is *The Holy Grail: Imagination and Belief* by Richard Barber (RB—no relation).[1] When one adds that the writer includes accounts of Williams's *War in Heaven* and the Taliessin poems the Williams enthusiast can really feel that his cup runneth over.

RB is qualified in several different ways for this work. Firstly, he is not an academic who, as he points out, would have an academic reputation to worry about. Secondly, unlike so many who venture into this field, he is scholarly, reading his texts in the original and citing his sources. Thirdly, he is a professional writer who has already written numerous books on Arthur and related matters. Fourthly, he has earned his living as a publisher, indeed, managing director of Boydell and Brewer, in which capacity he has edited a long series of Arthurian Studies, which have included not only translations of some of the key texts previously unavailable in English, but also Dodds's edition of Williams's Taliessin poems, as well as the other volume under review which I shall come to. Finally, he is modest: he has not only not mentioned these claims (apart from the first), but has also not published his own book but submitted it to another firm like anyone else.

Anyone who has dipped into Bruce's *The Development of Arthurian Romance* (one of Williams's sources) or Loomis's *Arthurian Literature in the Middle Ages* will know that the field is vast and trackless, more resembling the forest of Broceliande than normal scholarly territory. RB makes some simplifying assumptions, of which the key one is that the fundamental

---

1. Richard Barber, *The Holy Grail: Imagination and Belief* (London: Allen Lane, 2004).

texts are relatively few and all written within about forty years. The first is *The Story of the Grail*, begun by Chrétien de Troyes around 1190. This introduces the wounded king, the mysterious castle, the procession with the grail and the bleeding lance, and the unasked question. Chrétien did not live to finish his work, but his material was found so fascinating that twenty years later it was supplied with no fewer than four successive continuations and two prologues. There were no concepts of copyright or literary property in those days, and several important works were in fact composites by different hands. Then Robert de Boron supplied the grail with a history connecting it with Joseph of Arimathea. The *Perlesvaus* linked the grail more closely with the main Arthurian story. The material was incorporated into the composite work, which used to be known as the Vulgate Cycle but which has been renamed the Lancelot-Grail, after one major episode, the *Quest for the Holy Grail*. Our dear familiar English Malory comes at the end of this process and, from the point of view of sources, though not of course of literary merit, is late and derivative.

RB handles all this material with refreshing clarity, quoting key passages from the originals and showing how the grail became a dish, a cup and a chalice, sometimes in the same work at different times. Then he goes on to consider its links to the cult of relics, as the grail and the bleeding lance associated with it are supposed to be relics of the Passion. He also considers the developing cult of the eucharist, the increased ceremonial of the mass, and the institution of the feast of Corpus Christi, all associated with the same time and place as the French grail romances. His key point is that the grail is not a single thing but a literary concept, one which symbolizes a spiritual as well as a chivalric meaning and one which is deliberately veiled. But this section of his work abounds with insights, too many even to summarize. Here are just two: he suggests that too little attention is given to the historical context of scholarship. He also argues that Welsh nationalism was responsible for suggesting that Peredur in the Mabinogion was earlier than Chrétien, whereas he considers it is later. With this goes the whole edifice of Celtic origins, to which Loomis was so wedded, and which, incidentally, Williams rejected. He deals similarly with the idea that any episode in a later romance formed part of a jigsaw which, if only completed, would lead to the discovery of a lost original.

In the final section he considers modern versions of the grail legends. I want only to say that there is an extensive treatment of Williams. *War in Heaven* he finds enjoyable but somewhat dated, but he gives high praise to the Taliessin poems, which he expounds accurately, arguing that Williams made his own myth and used the legend as the mould for his individual and intensely Christian philosophy. There is also much else, which I do not have space to touch on.

As a footnote to this, Nigel Bryant's *The Legend of the Grail* is a valuable project.[2] This is

---

2. Nigel Bryant, *The Legend of the Holy Grail* (Martlesham: D. S. Brewer, 2004).

not a retelling, but rather a reworking of the relevant parts of the original French material—which Bryant has previously translated—into a single consistent story. It is therefore not like a normal modern retelling, such as those by Roger Lancelyn Green or Rosemary Sutcliff, and should rather be compared to Joseph Bédier's reconstruction of the Tristan story from the surviving sources. I have to say that I found it rather heavy going, but then of the medievals I prefer Wolfram and Malory, and of the moderns Wagner and Williams, to the French stories which started the whole thing off. But Bryant can claim to have given a single coherent and consistent account of what the French stories were getting at, without their endless digressions.

HERACLITUS ON THE WAY OF EXCHANGE

Bishop Kallistos Ware once[1] memorably described Williams's account of heaven as the place of exchange. He summed it up by drawing on a phrase Williams quotes in 'Bors to Elayne: on the King's Coins':

> This is the way of this world in the day of that other's;
> make yourselves friends by means of the riches of iniquity,
> for the wealth of the self is the health of the self exchanged.
> What saith Heracleitus? — and what is the City's breath? —
> *dying each other's life, living each other's death.*
> Money is a medium of exchange.
> ('Bors to Elayne: on the King's Coins,' 87-9)

In one of his few notes, Williams gives his source: 'The quotation from Heracleitus was taken from Mr. Yeats's book, *A Vision*.'[2]

This is a little terse, and it is worth following through in more detail. Heracleitus or Heraclitus[3] was one of the early Greek philosophers known to modern scholars as the pre-Socratics, and even in antiquity he was celebrated for his obscurity. This is compounded by the fact that, as with many others, his book survives only in quotations made by later writers, so what

---

1. 'Heaven and Hell in Charles Williams.' Unpublished paper given on 21 June 2003 to the Charles Williams Society.
2. Williams, *Taliessin through Logres* (Oxford: Oxford University Press), 95.
3. Heraclitus is the usual spelling by English scholars and I shall use it except in quotations.

is published under his name is a collection of fragments. In any case his book may well have been a collection of sayings, rather than a treatise. These gnomic utterances are very striking, as is clear from a few examples, including the original of the passage used by Yeats and Williams: [4]

The sun is new every day. (32; 6)

You cannot step twice into the same rivers; for fresh waters are ever flowing in upon you. (41, 42; 49a, 12)

War is the father of all and the king of all; and some he has made gods and some men, some bound and some free. (44; 53)

The immortals are mortal, the mortals immortal, each living in the others' death and dying in the others' life. (67; 62)

Fire lives the death of earth, and air lives the death of fire; water lives the death of air, earth that of water. (25; 76)

Although the Word is common to all, many live as if they had a private wisdom of their own. (92; 2)

The way up and the way down are one and the same. (69; 60)

Yeats came across Heraclitus in 1909, when he recorded the third and fourth of those above in his Journal.[5] It is clear from verbal similarities that he used a then standard work, John Burnet's *Early Greek Philosophy*, 1892 (the edition Yeats used[6]). Burnet was Professor of Greek at St Andrews University, and his book remained a standard source for English-speaking students for sixty years.[7]

Yeats did not publish this Journal, but the final phrase of the fragment, in the form 'dying

---

4. The following fragments are given first with the number in Burnet's edition (see reference 7 below); then the standard Diels-Kranz references, each of which should be prefixed with DK22b. The translations have been slightly modified. Eliot in 'Burnt Norton' (see note 31 below) used Diels' first edition of 1903. The 1952 fifth edition revised by Walther Kranz provides the still standard numbering system.
5. Yeats: *Memoirs*, transcribed and edited by Denis Donoghue (London: Macmillan, 1972), 216.
6. Harper and Hood demonstrate this convincingly in the notes to their edition (see reference 13 below), 32-3.
7. I have a 1952 reprint of the 1930 fourth edition (London: A. & C. Black). In 1957 it was superseded by G. S. Kirk and J. E. Raven: *The PreSocratic Philosophers* (Cambridge: Cambridge University Press). Burnet's edition of Plato is still widely used.

the other's life, living the other's death', became an obsession with him in his middle years. One could say that it plays a comparable part in his thought to that of 'This also is Thou; neither is this Thou' in Williams.[8] It occurs in several different places and is alluded to in more, but since Williams specifically cites *A Vision*, let us look at that.

A Vision is Yeats's book of occult wisdom. It was first published in 1925, in an edition of 600 signed copies 'privately printed for subscribers only.' It was therefore not an easy book to find, and it is a testimony to Williams's interest in Yeats that he did obtain it and praised it in his 1930 essay on Yeats as 'that learned and profound work.'[9] Yeats later revised it considerably, and the later version was published in 1937 in a normal edition. Yeats scholars distinguish the two editions as *Vision A* and *Vision B*. Williams reviewed *Vision B* when it appeared,[10] to Yeats's pleasure,[11] but it was *Vision A* which first engaged him.[12]

The phrase which interested him occurs first in one of Yeats's characteristic discussions of gyres, those interpenetrating cones which occur only in discussions of Yeats, but there turn up all the time. After a particularly tangled and abstruse passage we come across:

> It is as though the first act of being, after creating limit, was to divide itself into male and female, each dying the other's life living the other's death.[13]

This was considerably revised in *Vision B*, but the phrase is used again, and this time is attributed:

> Here the thought of Heraclitus dominates all: "Dying each other's life, living each other's death."[14] (*Vision B*, 68)

The second occurrence is in the context of Yeats's exposition of his cyclical theory of history, where we find:

---

8. E.g., *The Descent of the Dove* (London: Faber, 1950), viii. First published 1939; *The Figure of Beatrice* (London: Faber), 1943, 8.
9. Williams, *Poetry at Present* (Oxford: Oxford University Press), 1930, 58.
10. 'Staring at miracle,' *Time and Tide* 4 December 1937; reprinted in Williams, *The Celian Moment and other essays* (Carterton: The Greystones Press, 2017).
11. Foster, R. F.: *W. B. Yeats: A Life. II: The Arch-Poet* (Oxford: Oxford University Press, 2003,) 607.
12. *A Vision*, in either version, is notoriously obscure. To anyone wishing to study it in detail I recommend Northrop Frye: 'The Rising of the Moon,' in *Spiritus Mundi* (Bloomington: Indiana University Press, 1976), and Graham Hough: *The Mystery Religion of W. B. Yeats* (Hassocks: Harvester Press, 1984).
13. W. B. Yeats, *Vision A*, 130. I have used the reissue with introduction and notes by George Mills Harper and Walter Kelly Hood (London: Macmillan, 1978). The body of the book is a facsimile reprint of the original, with unchanged pagination.
14. Yeats, *A Vision* (*Vision B*) (London: Macmillan, 1937), 68.

> Each age unwinds the thread another age had wound, and it amuses one to remember that before Phidias, and his westward moving art, Persia fell, and that when full moon came round again, amid eastward moving thought, and brought Byzantine glory, Rome fell; and that at the outset of our eastward moving Renaissance Byzantium fell; all things dying each other's life, living each other's death (*Vision A*, 183= *Vision B*, 270-1).

Williams seems to have picked up the phrase, without engaging with the Platonic content of the first half of the sentence in the first version. With the second sentence all readers of the Taliessin poems will find resonances with Yeats's mention of Byzantine glory and the significance of Rome and, to a lesser extent, Persia, while noting that Yeats's cyclical theory of history makes no appeal to Williams as a Christian.

Since Yeats did not attribute the phrase to Heraclitus in *Vision A*, how did Williams know where it came from? It seems unlikely that 'Bors to Elayne' was written after 1937, when *Vision B* was published, given that *Taliessin through Logres* came out in 1938 and Anne Ridler dated most of the poems in it to 1934-5.[15] One possibility is that he picked it up from Yeats's play *The Resurrection*, whose closing words, before a song, are:

> Your words are clear at last, O Heraclitus. God and man die each other's life, live each other's death.[16]

However, I prefer to think that Williams simply asked Yeats, whom he knew personally.[17] This would account for his use of the variant spelling Heracleitus, which is slightly closer to the Greek.

To consider in detail the significance of this phrase to Yeats would take us too far afield, so one passage must suffice:

> To me all things are made of the conflict of two states of consciousness, beings or persons which die each other's life, live each other's death. This is true of life and death themselves.[18]

The significance of the phrase to Williams is clear. It is a summary of the way of exchange. In 'Bors to Elayne: on the King's Coins' it is spoken by the archbishop, so his acceptance of a Greek saying implies the acceptance by Christianity of what is good and true in paganism.

---

15. Introduction to Williams: *The Image of the City* (Oxford: Oxford University Press, 1958), lxiii, footnote.
16. Yeats: *Collected Plays* (London: Macmillan, 1952), 594. The play, in a version which includes this passage, was first published in 1931.
17. A. M. Hadfield: *Charles Williams: An Exploration of his Life and Work* (Oxford: Oxford University Press, 1983), 31.
18. Yeats: *Letters*, edited Allan Wade (London: Rupert Hart Davis, 1954), 917.

We may compare St Paul's quotation of a line of the Greek poet Aratus,[19] and Williams would also have been aware that he was thought to have quoted Euripides.[20]

Williams uses the line again in 'The Founding of the Company,' again to summarize the way of exchange:

> The Company's second mode bore farther
> the labour and fruition; it exchanged the proper self
> and wherever need was drew breath daily
> in another's place, according to the grace of the Spirit
> 'dying each other's life, living each other's death'.
> ('The Founding of the Company,' 60-4)

The most dramatic example of exchange in the poems is Blanchefleur, who, we know from Malory, 'died from a letting of blood to heal a sick lady.'[21] In 'The Last Voyage', her body accompanies Galahad to Sarras:

> Before the helm the ascending-descending sun
> lay in quadrilateral covers of a saffron pall
> over the bier and the pale body of Blanchefleur,
> mother of the nature of lovers, creature of exchange;
> drained there of blood by the thighed wound,
> she died another's death, another lived her life.
> ('The Last Voyage,' 70-4)

Furthermore, exchange may operate not only among the living, but also, with due qualifications, in respect of the dead. We remember Pauline Anstruther in *Descent into Hell*, and, more immediately, 'Taliessin on the Death of Virgil.'

By virtue of his fourth eclogue, which was considered to foretell the birth of Christ—and indeed did so, if we allow that poets may speak more wisely than they know[22]—Virgil was considered a prophet, 'Maro, prophet of the gentiles.' But as a pagan, who had not faith, he did not know grace and his place in the afterlife was in limbo, from which he is sent to rescue Dante, who was in an even worse predicament.[23] 'Others he saved; himself he could not save':

---

19. Acts 17: 28.
20. Milton, Introduction to *Samson Agonistes*, citing I Cor 15.33.
21. Malory, *Le Morte Darthur*, XVII. 11.
22. The principle is as old as Plato's *Ion*.
23. *Inferno*, opening.

this line from the gospel accounts of the Passion,[24] which Williams uses to sum up Virgil's predicament in the poem, is also the starting point for his principal prose exposition of exchange,[25] and the first of his sentences 'For the Companions of the Co-inherence.'[26] And Virgil's friends, that is, in principle, all of those who have recognized great poetry and followed the prophecy which he unwittingly made, can take part in Virgil's redemption by prayer across time and the barrier of death. Williams is here applying to Virgil himself the general law of the spiritual life which he used Heraclitus's words to enunciate, and which Dante's Virgil helped him to understand.[27]

Williams went on to use the phrase to summarise the way of exchange in two of his plays. In *The Death of Good Fortune* we find this dialogue:

> *The Lover*
> Master, though your knowledge fails, you are not unwise.
> Which of us two is true?
>
> *The Magician*
> Either; go you
> living in death and he dying in life.
> Toss for your choice.[28]

In *The House of the Octopus*, there is the following speech by the Flame:

> This is the mind of the church—
> to discover always the way of the lover and the lover.
> The young shall save the old and the old the young,
> the dead the living and the other living the dead
> and my tongue shall tell in heaven the truth of all.[29]

---

24. It occurs in all three synoptic gospels: Matt. 27.42; Mark 15.31; Luke 23.35.
25. *He Came Down from Heaven* (London: Faber, 1950), 83. First published 1938, the same year as *Taliessin through Logres*.
26. Hadfield: *Charles Williams*, 174.
27. In Dante's own scheme Virgil is seen trapped in limbo and has no access to purgatory except as an observer. Williams sees exchange operating not only between the living and the dead but also backwards in time, as indeed it sometimes does in Dante too (Casella in *Purgatorio* II, Trajan in *Paradiso* XX). We must also remember that Dante's poem does not purport to give us a definitive account of the afterlife but a vision of it, imagined to suit the needs of Dante the character in the poem.
28. Williams, *Collected Plays* (Oxford: Oxford University Press, 1963, 189.
29. *ibid*. 310.

To conclude this discussion, we can consider C. S. Lewis's brief mention of this passage, which comes in his discussion of that part of Williams's obscurity which he ascribes to Unshared Backgrounds. He compares Williams's requirements with those of T. S. Eliot in *The Waste Land* and starts by arguing that some of each poet's expectations are wholly legitimate. He goes on:

> When Mr. Eliot assumes that you know Miss Weston's *From Ritual to Romance*, or Williams that you know Heracleitus as quoted by W. B. Yeats . . . the difficulties are becoming less obviously legitimate.[30]

This is a good debating point: the implication is that Williams has not only used a secondary source but one which may have distorted the original author's meaning. We should also remember that at the time Lewis was writing, Yeats's occult interests, as embodied in *A Vision* and elsewhere, did not have the fashionable New Age aura that attends similar interests now. They were then highly disreputable. For example, W. H. Auden wrote an obituary dialogue for Yeats in which he puts this jibe into the mouth of an imaginary Public Prosecutor:

> In 1900 he [Yeats] believed in fairies; that was bad enough; but in 1930 we are confronted with the pitiful, the deplorable spectacle of a grown man occupied with the mumbo-jumbo of magic and the nonsense of India.[31]

No, if one were going to quote Heraclitus, much better to do so from an unimpeachable source. Lewis might have remembered that, two years before *Taliessin through Logres* was published, Eliot had published 'Burnt Norton'[32] and had prefixed it with two epigraphs from Heraclitus—but these were in the original Greek, and quoted, not second-hand from Yeats, nor even from Burnet's handbook, but from the scholar's reference work, the German edition by Diels. Eliot's epigraphs are the last two of the seven passages I quoted at the beginning of this paper.

However, Lewis's is not more than a debating point: Yeats's version is perfectly accurate as far as the immediate sense of his original is concerned, and Burnet is a respectable source. What Heraclitus himself meant by it is anyone's guess—or rather, to put the same point more elegantly, it is a matter for controversy among scholars. Yeats seized on the passage, as poets

---

30. Williams and C. S. Lewis: *Arthurian Torso*, Oxford: Oxford University Press, 1948), 189.
31. W. H. Auden: 'The Public v. the Late Mr. William Butler Yeats' in *The English Auden*, edited Edward Mendelson, (London: Faber, 1977), 391.
32. 'Burnt Norton' first appeared at the end of Eliot's *Collected Poems 1909-1935* (London: Faber, 1936). When it was reissued as the first of *Four Quartets* (London: Faber, 1944), the epigraphs were transferred to prefix the whole cycle.

do, and incorporated it into his own imaginative vision. So did Williams. The moral is clear: whereas scholars should try to convey the sense of their originals and not distort them, it is the poet's privilege to convert what they appropriate, and the right test is not fidelity to the original but suitability to the new context. And Williams here uses Heraclitus's phrase to embody succinctly one of his central beliefs.

WILLIAMS AND THE SEA NYMPH

*I*n 'The Last Voyage' the ship of Solomon drives towards Sarras, and Williams uses two similes to characterize her motion. This paper is concerned with the first:

> as the fine fair arm of pine-changed Cymodocea,
> striking from the grey-green waters of tossed Tiber,
> thrust the worshipful duke to the rescue of Rome;
> (lines 58-60; *Taliessin through Logres*, page 86)

My aim is to write a gloss on this passage, but I need to make something of a voyage myself to get into a position to do so. Let us start with Cymodocea. (I read this with 'y' as in French 'u', both 'o's short, the 'c' hard, the stress on the 'e', 'ea' disyllabic; this is the 'reformed' pronunciation which Williams probably expected; but the 'traditional' pronunciation with a soft 'c' and the stress possibly on the second 'o' would also work.) In Greek mythology, this name belonged to a Nereid, one of the fifty daughters of the minor sea-god Nereus and the Okeanid Doris. Hesiod gives an account of them together with names for all fifty.[1] Many of these names express aspects of the sea; *Κυμοδόκη* (Kumodókē), to give her the Greek form of her name, means 'wave-receiver.' Homer gives a similar list, and she turns up there also.[2] The Nereids are sea-nymphs, who, like all nymphs, are female, semi-divine, long-lived though usually not immortal, and forever young. Nymphs are usually associated with a place or some

---

1. Hesiod, *Theogony*, 240-264.
2. *Iliad*, 18: 39.

part of nature. The function of the Nereids is chiefly to remain as a group, playing in the sea or dancing on the shore. A few of them have individual stories; the best known is Thetis, desired by Zeus but foretold to bear a son greater than his father. Zeus therefore reluctantly married her off to Peleus, a mortal. Their wedding is the main subject of Catullus's longest and most elaborate poem,[3] and their son was Achilles.

In the *Aeneid*, Virgil first introduces our sea-nymph, Latinizing her name, with some of the other Nereids as attendants of the sea-god Neptune, the Roman equivalent of Greek Poseidon, while the Trojans are sailing from Sicily to Cumae in Italy.[4] But it is the later use of her name that is relevant to Williams's passage, and by this time Virgil has used it in a different story.

In Book 9, the Trojan ships are under attack by Aeneas's enemy, Turnus. Cybele, the Phrygian mother-goddess, whom Virgil treats as mother of all the gods, had previously extracted an agreement from Jove, the equivalent of Zeus. This was that the ships, which had been built from pine trees from her sacred grove on mount Ida, should never be overcome, but that those which had completed the journey should be turned into sea-nymphs. When Turnus began his attack on the ships the promise was fulfilled.[5] This episode has been much criticized; it has been called 'the most incongruous episode in the whole *Aeneid*;'[6] it is much more the kind of story we would expect to find in Ovid, who does indeed use it.[7] However, what is clear is that these sea-nymphs, though like Nereids, are not Nereids, since they started life as pine trees, not daughters of Nereus;[8] they are not given individual names at this point.

Then in Book 10, we have Aeneas coming to the rescue of his comrades with a new fleet, which had been loaned him by the Etruscan king Tarchon. He meets the former ships of his own fleet, now sea-nymphs, and they dance around his ship in salute. One of them is a better talker than the rest. She is named as Cymodocea.[9] She therefore cannot be the same sea-nymph as appeared in Book 5: after all the present one was still a ship then and never was a Nereid. She has to be another sea-nymph with the same name. Virgil left the confusion unresolved—after all he left the poem unfinished and unrevised—or perhaps he liked the name so much that he used it twice, intending to change it in one of the places. Anyway, she warns Aeneas of the danger ahead and, on finishing, 'with a thrust of her right hand, she drove the

---

3. Catullus poem 64.
4. *Aeneid* 5: 826.
5. *Aeneid* 9: 80-122.
6. R. D. Williams (ed.), *The Aeneid of Virgil* (London: Macmillan, 1972-3, 2 vols.), II. 283-4. See also Gordon Williams, *Technique and Ideas in the Aeneid* (New Haven: Yale University Press, 1983), 128-9.
7. Ovid, *Metamorphoses* 14: 530-65
8. *Aeneid*, 9: 102-3.
9. *Aeneid* 10: 225.

ship upon its way' (*dixerat et dextra discedens impulit altam / haud ignara modi puppim*).¹⁰ This is the source of Cymodocea and her thrust of the ship in 'The Last Voyage'.

The translation of the Virgilian sentence I have just used is taken from Williams's own retelling, *The Story of the Aeneid*, published in 1936 while he was working on the poems of *Taliessin through Logres*. And there are other Virgilian echoes here. In the Introduction to his retelling he comments on Virgil's feeling for Nature: 'a feeling exact in its details, and yet laden with a content which is certainly not Wordsworthian, but from which Wordsworth might have learned.' He goes on: 'His river-gods (cf. Tiber, p. 95) and his sea-nymphs (p. 118) are neither rivers nor waves, and yet they are not merely gods inhabiting those places. A kind of strange life, inhuman, and yet aware of humanity, moves in them.'¹¹

I have left in his page references, because the second one is to this passage in Book 10 (I shall come to the first one shortly), and they also show Williams associating sea-nymphs with the Tiber as he does in our passage. In fact the Tiber is doubly relevant. Firstly, in Virgil Aeneas is still sailing down the coast when he meets the sea-nymphs and is given his helpful push. But in Williams he has already turned into the river Tiber before Cymodocea appears, and there is no mention of her companions. This compression of Virgil's story is followed by and indeed requires another. In the *Aeneid* Rome has not yet been founded and Aeneas is heading for the Trojan camp, which is near the river mouth.¹² However, Williams has him coming 'to the rescue of Rome,' which is, or rather will be, about thirty kilometres upstream. Aeneas is rescuing Rome in the sense of the idea of Rome or of the destiny of the descendants of the Trojans who will found it. Rome is an embodiment of the City for Williams in a way that the Trojan camp cannot be.

Moreover, Rome is suggested by mentioning the Tiber, on whose banks it will be built. But in describing Cymodocea as 'striking from the ... Tiber,' has Williams relocated their meeting upstream? The exact position of the Trojan camp is not easy to work out from the scattered references in Virgil's text. However, the matter is dealt with in Appendix F of J. W. Mackail's edition of the *Aeneid*. Mackail was the leading English Virgilian scholar of the time, and his edition was published in 1930 by the Oxford University Press, so Williams would have had ready access to it, and indeed referred to it in his introduction. Mackail provides a map and explains that 'On reaching the mouth of the Tiber .. the Trojan fleet rowed up the river for about a mile ... There they landed, and fortified a camp.'¹³ The next incident after the meeting with Cymodocea is that Aeneas sees the Trojan camp,¹⁴ so Williams clearly felt it legitimate for the meeting to be described as on the Tiber, although he may be considered as

---

10. *Aeneid* 10: 246-7.
11. Williams, *The Story of the Aeneid* (Oxford: Oxford University Press, 1936), Introduction, ix.
12. *Aeneid* 7: 35-6, 106.
13. J. W. Mackail (ed.), *Virgil: The Aeneid* (Oxford: Clarendon Press, 1930), 529.
14. *Aeneid* 10: 260.

having relocated it. I pass over the question of whether or how far sea-nymphs are permitted to go up rivers; since Cymodocea started life as—or in—a tree she would then presumably have been a Dryad; as a water nymph she would be a Naiad; the relocation to fresh water does not appear to bother her.

Secondly, Williams was clearly impressed by the passage in which Tiber the river-god appeared to Aeneas in a dream;[15] this is his first reference in the passage quoted from Williams's Introduction. His purpose was to advise Aeneas on how to find the future site of Rome, but for our passage it is his appearance rather than his prophecy that is important. He is described as 'clothed in a grey-green cloak', Williams's version of *eum tenuis glauco uelabat amictu / carbasus*.[16] This gives us the 'grey-green waters of tossed Tiber' in 'The Last Voyage.' The adjective *glaucus*, rendered by Williams as 'grey-green' is hard to translate; originally it meant 'gleaming' but later it came to be used for the colour of rivers and the sea; translators usually render it as 'grey'.

How much of all this does the reader need or want to know? Cymodocea's message of warning is not relevant, nor the use of her name for two different nymphs, nor the issue of the site of the Trojan camp, nor the possible relocation of the meeting with Cymodocea from the sea to the river Tiber, nor the origin of the phrase 'grey-green.' Sources are not meaning, and much of this is irrelevant to Williams's meaning. This article is long already, but even so, with heroic restraint I have refrained from exploring other fascinating byways, such as other appearances of Nereids in Greek literature, Virgil's apparently earliest reference to Cymodocea in the *Georgics*, which is generally agreed to be an interpolation,[17] his echo of the opening of Catullus's poem, the potential confusion with Cymothoe, who really is a Nereid,[18] or sundry allusions to the Virgilian passages in other English poets.

Meanwhile, what gloss, containing only the essentials and omitting the detailed Virgilian references, would I offer for the passage? The following is, I suggest, the minimum, adding a few points for completeness:

> 58-60: the headlong rush of the ship is compared to the speed of Aeneas's ship as he rushes to the relief of his comrades, besieged by Turnus. *Cymodocea*: a sea-nymph. Her *fine fair arm*: Williams regularly sees a woman's arm as embodying her beauty, as in 'The Coming of Palomides.' *pine-changed*: in the *Aeneid*, Cymodocea was originally one of a group of pine trees in a sacred grove on Mount Ida, from which Aeneas's original fleet was built; they were turned into sea-nymphs by Jove to avoid their being burned by Turnus; he was lent a new fleet by the Etruscans. *Tiber*: the river on which Rome will be built. *thrust*: Cymodocea gave Aeneas's ship a

---

15. *Aeneid* 8: 31-65.
16. *Aeneid* 8: 33-4.
17. *Georgics* 4: 338.
18. *Aeneid* 1: 144.

push which gave it great speed. *worshipful duke*: Aeneas: his constant epithet is *pius*, which is hard to translate, but implies a combination of 'faithful' and 'devout' for which *worshipful* is an equivalent; *duke* is a descendant of the Latin *dux*, a military commander. *Rome*: in relieving the Trojan camp Aeneas looks forward to the future city.

However, personally I find the poem illuminated by exploring something of Williams's use of Virgil and his admiration of Virgil's feeling for Nature.

A DEBT TO GEORGE ELIOT?

In George Eliot's *The Mill on the Floss*, Stephen Guest notices Maggie Tulliver's arm:

> Who has not felt the beauty of a woman's arm? The unspeakable suggestions of tenderness that lie in the dimpled elbow, and all the varied gently-lessening curves, down to the delicate wrist, with its tiniest, almost imperceptible nicks in the firm softness. A woman's arm touched the soul of a great sculptor two thousand years ago so that he wrought an image of it for the Parthenon which moves us still as it clasps lovingly the time-worn marble of a headless trunk. Maggie's was such an arm as that—and it had the warm tints of life.[1]

Note the hint of the divine, achieved by a comparison of Maggie's arm with Phidias's statue of the goddess Athene. For all that she was a freethinker, George Eliot clearly understood the way in which the loved person carries, or seems to carry, a sense of being unfallen, even divine. Williams does something very similar in *Shadows of Ecstasy*, when Philip notices Rosamond's arm:

> Well, after all, Rosamond was only human; she couldn't be absolutely perfect. And then as she stretched out her arm again he cried out that she was perfect, she was more than perfect; the movement of her arm was something frightfully important, and now it was gone. He had seen

---

1. George Eliot, *The Mill on the Floss*, Book 6, Chapter 10 'The Spell seems Broken.'

the verge of a great conclusion of mortal things and then it had vanished. Over that white curve he had looked into incredible space; abysses of intelligence lay beyond it.[2]

In both cases it is the beloved's arm which gives a moment of visionary experience with a divine aura playing about it.

Williams returned to this image in *Taliessin through Logres*, when Palomides sees Iseult's arm:

> I saw the hand of the queen Iseult;
> down her arm a ruddy bolt
> fired the tinder of my brain
> to measure the shape of man again.[3]

And the queen's arm becomes 'a rigid bar of golden flame' in Palomides's reflection and analysis of what has happened. These are examples of the Beatrician experience, which Williams expounds and analyzes so memorably in *The Figure of Beatrice*. And there is a related reflection in *Witchcraft*: 'one will be with a lover and the hand will become a different and terrifying thing . . . a phenomenon, being wholly itself, is laden with universal meaning.'[4]

In her second book on Williams, Alice Mary Hadfield gives a long list of the writers Williams read as part of his editorial work at the Oxford University Press.[5] George Eliot does not appear in this list, but in fact the Press reissued her novels in the 1920s in the World's Classics series, and he might have read them then, if he had not done so before. The only discussion of her work that I can recall comes in the Preface to his anthology, *A Book of Victorian Narrative Verse*, in which he sees her as embodying nobility, and briefly mentions three of her novels, of which *The Mill on the Floss* is one.[6]

Of course the book is hardly an obscure one. Moreover, Williams was capable of alighting on the image of a woman's arm as being revelatory for himself. But I wonder whether there was a specific indebtedness.

---

2. Charles Williams, *Shadows of Ecstasy*, Chapter 4 'The Majesty of the King.'
3. Charles Williams, *Taliessin through Logres*, 'The Coming of Palomides.'
4. Charles Williams, *Witchcraft*, 77-8.
5. *Charles Williams: An Exploration of his Life and Work* (New York: Oxford University Press, 1983), 77.
6. Charles Williams (ed.), *A Book of Victorian Narrative Verse* (Oxford: Clarendon Press, 1927), iii-v.

PEOPLE AND PLACES
IN THE TALIESSIN POEMS
A REGISTER AND GAZETTEER

INTRODUCTORY NOTE

The aim of these lists is to supply the background information assumed by the poems, but not to repeat what is in them. They are intended to be comprehensive for named people and places. The notes give only what is relevant to the poems. Sometimes this means stating the obvious, but this implies that the obvious meaning is the right one; of course I could be mistaken. The sources of this information are variously: general reference works; works in and on the Arthurian tradition in general, and in particular the *Mabinogion*[1] and Malory;[2] commentaries on Williams. Passages taken or adapted from Williams's own notes and other comments on the poems are in quotation marks without attribution; these sometimes give details not incorporated into poems and are subject to the usual warning about poets interpreting themselves. They come from a variety of sources: the end-notes to *Taliessin through Logres*, the *Preface* to *The Region of the Summer Stars*; *The Figure of Arthur*;[3] essays and notes collected in *The Image of the City* and *The Celian Moment*; Williams's *Notes for C. S. Lewis*; and the oral explanations recorded by his friends, notably Lewis and Alice Mary Hadfield; and the

---

1. Williams used Lady Charlotte Guest's translation, first published 1849, and frequently reprinted. I used the old Everyman edition (Dent, 1906). Guest includes one story, 'Taliesin,' not included in more recent versions; Williams also drew on Guest's extensive notes.
2. Williams read Malory in editions based on Caxton's text, with Caxton's chapter divisions and title *Le Morte Darthur*. Editions based on the Winchester manuscript and titled *The Works of Thomas Malory* were not published until after his death.
3. Williams's book is referred to as FA; references to Lewis's commentary are noted as AT.

Notes published by the Charles Williams Society. Although strictly speaking these enjoy descending levels of authority, in practice it seems simplest to run them together. A full annotated edition of the poems would identify every source separately but that seems unnecessarily elaborate for this purpose. Passages from Williams's other books are separately identified.[4]

PEOPLE IN THE TALIESSIN POEMS: A REGISTER OF NAMES

This is intended to be comprehensive for named people, but slaves and others whose names are not given, notably the Prophet of Islam, and the headless emperor of P'o-l'u, are not listed (I have made an exception for Aeneas). Family relationships and other points assumed by the poems are given according to the Arthurian tradition in general and Malory in particular. A general comment by Williams is also helpful: 'The knights are capacities of man and modes of being (but also knights).'

Adam by / 'The Adam' Williams refers to both Adam and Eve.

Aeneas / The founder of Rome, not named but the 'worshipful duke' of 'The Last Voyage.' 'Worshipful' because of his constant epithet of *pius*, which is more than English *pious*: 'It is the honourable fulfilment of all moral duties.' 'Duke' represents Latin *dux*, a military leader.

Agravaine / Third son of Lot and Morgause; with his brother Gawaine he exposes Lancelot's relationship with Guinevere and also murders Morgause and Lamorack.

Ala-ud-Dina / Common name for rulers in various parts of Asia.

Archimedes / Greek mathematician and scientist of the third century B.C., particularly influential on Arabic work.

Arthur / 'Man loving himself and hating himself. The fatality, the curse, the result of the Dolorous Blow, has to work itself out through the King;' 'Arthur unknowingly committed incest with his sister Morgause, who became by him the mother of Mordred.'

Augustus / Following the battle of Actium in 31 B.C. Octavian became master of the Roman

---

[4]. Note the abbreviations DD for *The Descent of the Dove* (London: Faber), 1950 (first published Longmans 1939)) and FB for *The Figure of Beatrice* (London: Faber, 1943).

world, with the name of emperor; he took the title Augustus in 27 B.C. He was responsible for commissioning the *Aeneid* from Virgil.

Balan / Balin's younger brother.

Balin / Knight of the two swords; 'after the dolorous blow struck against King Pelles in Carbonek by Balin the Savage, Balin and Balan his brother killed each other unknowingly.'

Bedivere / Brother to Kay; one of Arthur's original companions and also the last remaining following the last battle; he was charged with flinging the sword Excalibur into the lake.

Blanchefleur / Percivale's sister and a princess; the preeminent example in the poems of substitution in Williams's sense; 'Blanchefleur died from a letting of blood to heal a sick lady' (Malory XVII. 11); in *The Region* she is known as Dindrane and Williams says she 'was called Blanchfleur [*sic*] in religion' ('The Calling of Taliessin' 376; cf. Lewis in *AT* 138).[5]

Bors / 'The nephew of Lancelot and the companion of Galahad and Percivale' [in achieving the Grail]; 'the ordinary man, married, with children, the King's servant. But he is also the spiritual intellect concerned, as it must be, with earthly things.'

Brisen / Daughter of Nimue; Space; Helayne's nurse.

Catullus / Roman poet, *floruit* 61-54 B.C.; rejected lover of Lesbia.

Ceridwen / Taliessin's mother; goddess of nature in Welsh mythology; she was preparing a cauldron of inspiration; her servant Gwion of Bach tasted three drops which gave him the ability to foretell the future; after a shape-changing pursuit she swallowed him but later he was reborn from her; she wrapped the infant in a leathern bag or coracle and cast him into the sea.

Charon / Guardian of the underworld and ferryman of the dead in classical mythology (e.g. *Aeneid*, VI. 298ff.) and also in Dante's *Inferno*, III. 83ff.

Circe / In classical mythology Circe was a witch who turned her visitors into animals until

---

5. Williams's spelling is not consistent: it is Blanchefleur in *Taliessin through Logres* (seven occurrences), also in *The Image of the City*, 179; it is Blanchfleur once in *The Region of the Summer Stars*, as noted, and five times in the posthumous *Figure of Arthur*. The earlier form seems the better attested and also the more logical: the name derives from Chrétien's Blancheflor. See 'A note on the text of the Taliessin poems.'

overcome by Odysseus (Homer, *Odyssey*, X; Virgil, *Aeneid*, VII); her son is the enchanter Comus (revelry) who appears in Milton.

Coelius Vibenna / 'a leader of the Etruscans when they once occupied Rome. They were said to be great in black magic; hence "Etruscan spells."'

Cradlemas / King of London before Arthur.[6]

Cymodocea / One of the Nereids, the fifty sea-nymphs who were daughters of Nereus, mentioned in *Aeneid* V. 826. Her name means 'wave-receiver', or, as Hesiod puts it: she 'easily calms the waves upon the misty seas and the blasts of raging winds' (*Theogony*, 252, 1914 Loeb edition).

Deodatus / Pope; historically there were two popes named Adeodatus in the relevant period, but this pope is Williams's invention.

Dinadan / 'Dinadan realizes that loss may be a greater possession than having; and Palomides, who would be incapable of believing believingly believes unbelievingly, by means of that more-than-irony.'

Dindrane / Alternative name for Blanchefleur.

Dubric / Archbishop of Caerleon and primate of England.

Elayne / Bors's wife; 'nor is it by chance that the name of Bors's wife in Malory is that of the Grail-princess without the rough breathing: Elayne and Helayne.'

Emperor / Ruler of the empire from Byzantium; 'operative providence;' 'God-in-operation or God-as-known-by-man; Fate; operative force—as and according to the person concerned, but mostly here the God relation;' 'in the East there appeared the succession of almost pontiff-emperors in the new Rome' (DD, 74).

Elphin / He rescued the infant cast away by Ceridwen, named him Taliessin and cared for him.

---

6. Although Williams wrote to Lewis 'the name was meant for Cradlement [Malory I. 14]; that was a pure slip,' Cradlemas appears in Malory I. 12, and Williams used this form both earlier and later (Dodds' edition, 168, 283-5).

Euclid / Greek mathematician of around 300 B.C. whose *Elements* was studied by the Arabs and remained a fundamental textbook of geometry into the modern era.

Galahad / Son of Lancelot by Helayne; 'man's capacity for Christ, or—to avoid dogma—let us say, for divine things;' 'that in the human soul which finds Christ;' 'Arthur and Guinevere and Lancelot have all been talking about love, and this is the result, as it always is. We get Galahad instead of what we wanted;' 'He is flesh and blood in the union with the Flesh and the Blood' (DD, 117); also referred to as Merciful Childe, High Prince and Infant.

Gareth / Fourth son of Lot and Morgause; he came to Arthur's court in disguise and was set to work in the kitchen.

Garlon / Brother of Pelles; king of Castle Mortal; 'it was through the quarrel with him that Balin the Savage came to strike the dolorous blow at Pelles' with the sacred Lance; 'the Invisible Knight—who is Satan to us but the Holy Ghost to the supernatural powers;' appears unnamed in 'Taliessin at Lancelot's Mass,' 23, and is identified in Williams's end note.

Gawaine / Eldest son of Lot and Morgause; 'the kind of man who is very keen on the honour of his house and his own honour and proper dignity. He is a charming creature, so long as everyone looks up to him and gives way to him;' 'worldly honour run mad;' with his brother Agravaine he exposes Lancelot's relationship with Guinevere and also murders Morgause and Lamorack.

Guinevere / Arthur's queen; 'Arthur at first just thinks Guinevere would be a convenient adjunct of his royalty.'

Gwyddno / Father of Elphin.

Helayne / Daughter of Pelles and mother of Galahad by Lancelot; 'Galahad's mother who knew no images has to be subordinated to Lancelot, and Lancelot who was devoted to an image has to be cheated of it; and so a kind of grand substitution is worked out in the dark chamber—each becoming either on that plane, as the Seed is worked out on another' (ICW 190); 'mother of achievement.'

Henwg / Reputed father of Taliessin in versions given in notes to Guest's *Mabinogion*.

Heracleitus / Greek philosopher of the pre-Socratic period (around 500 B.C.), famous for his obscurity.

Iseult / Wife of Mark and lover of Tristram.

John / John saw *Revelation* on the island of Patmos.

Julius Cæsar / His two expeditions to Britain were in 55 and 54 B.C.

Kay / Arthur's steward; brother to Bedivere.

Lamorack / 'Brother of Percivale and Blanchefleur. He was the lover of the queen Morgause of Orkney, Arthur's sister. The two were killed by her sons, Gawaine and Agravaine, for the honour of the house of Orkney'; 'Lamorack's love affair is more a matter of terrible fate than Lancelot's.'

Lancelot / Friend of Arthur; lover of Guinevere; 'eighth in succession from Christ (8 is the number of the Christhood), and of his blood; the strongest and greatest knight alive (person as distinguished from office); much more than Arthur concerned with love as a thing of dolour and labour and vision.' 'It is he who is mostly concerned with choosing necessity (which is the subject of all great poetry).'

Lesbia / Catullus's love.

Levi / Among the Israelites the tribe of priests; in 'The Death of Palomides,' Kabbalists.

Lleon of Lochlin / Guest's Taliesin says: 'I have been bard of the harp to Lleon of Lochlin' (*Mabinogion*, 274); Williams makes Taliessin a fighting man as well as a poet.

Lot / King of Orkney, husband of Morgause.

Manes / Alternative form of Mani (216-276 A.D.), a Babylonian prophet; he preached a dualistic religion known as Manichaeism which Williams, following western tradition, treats as a heretical form of Christianity; it had reached Spain by the fourth century; 'The new heresy of Manichaeism which was intruding from the East might indeed exclude matter and the world from its consideration. But the orthodox Faith, based on the union of very matter with very deity, could not do so' (DD, 45).

Mark / King of Cornwall, husband of Iseult and uncle of Tristram.

Mars / Roman god of war.

Mary-in-blessing / Virgin Mary.

Mary Magdalene / Traditionally identified with the unnamed woman who anointed Christ's feet in *Luke* VII.

Merlin / Magician who watches over Arthur's early life; son of Nimue; 'time and the high prophetic intelligence of the world "brooding on things to come."'

Mordred / Son of Arthur and Morgause by incest who later led a rebellion against his father; 'entire egotism, Arthur's self-attention carried to the final degree.'

Morgause / Arthur's half-sister; wife of Lot of Orkney; mother of Gawaine, Gaheris, Agravaine, Gareth, and also by incest of Mordred; lover of Lamorack; later killed by Gaheris.

Nero / Fifth Roman emperor; ruled 54-68 A.D..

Nestorius / Patriarch of Constantinople (Byzantium) and heretic (fourth century); he 'declared that there were in Christ two beings united by a moral union and not one divine Person' (*Descent of the Dove*, 70); he also denied that the Virgin Mary was *theotokos* (mother of God) and *anthropotokos* (mother of man); his teaching was condemned at the Council of Ephesus, 431.

Nimue / 'Nimue is holy undefiled Nature—Creation outside man;' 'the Nature of Creation as the mother of Merlin (Time) and Brisen (Space); the source of movement and distance. She is almost the same state represented by the Emperor's Court, but more vast, dim, and aboriginal;' 'mother of making;' Merlin and Brisen are twins: 'children of some high parthenogenetical birth of Nimue in Broceliande.'

Palomides / Saracen prince who joins Arthur's court; 'the knight who begins by believing in good and evil almost (as so many do) as two separate origins and powers. He is, like most of us, a dualist. He then becomes a Mahommedan and believes in one control. He then becomes a Christian and believes in reconciliation, transmutation, and Unity. Also, he is especially man combating and overcoming sex (the Blatant Beast). He is in some sense an image and shadow of Galahad, for it is significant that he is baptized (after his conquest) on the day when Galahad comes to the King's hall.'

Paul / St Paul; his visit to Athens is recorded in Acts XVII: 23; obliquely referred to in *Prelude to The Region*, 12; the cathedral in London is dedicated to him.

Pelles / King of Carbonek; keeper of the Grail and other hallows, notably the sacred spear or lance; the Wounded King; victim of the Dolorous Blow.

Pendragon / A title meaning a chief leader from *pen* (head) and *dragwn* (dragon, leader).

Percivale / Brother of Blanchefleur; 'at once Taliessin in his highest degree, and a virginal lover (because he and Blanchefleur have no time for anything else); but also the spiritual intellect concerned with the significance of things and with the Quest;' 'the imagination of the other [world] and of the universe; he is the brother of Blanchefleur =substitution.'

Pheilippides / Messenger who brought the news of the victory at Marathon to Athens and who died of exhaustion after doing so. (Pheidippides, who sought help by the Athenians from the Spartans before the battle, was later identified with this man, but Williams's spelling was an accepted variant.)

Phœbus / Apollo's title as sun-god (*phoibos* means radiant); Apollo was the god of music and poetry.

Rhea Silvia / Roman vestal virgin (priestess), descendant of Aeneas, raped by the god Mars and mother of the twins Romulus and Remus; she was imprisoned and they were exposed but saved by being suckled by a wolf; Romulus later became founder of Rome (*Aeneid* I. 275 and VII. 659).

Solomon / Israelite king.

Stephen / First martyr and dedicatee of the cathedral in Camelot.

Talaat ibn Kula / Either Williams's invention or a free rendering of Thabit ibn Qurrah, an Arabic mathematician (836-901) who translated Greek mathematical works.

Taliessin / Arthur's poet; the name means Radiant Brow; 'the poetic imagination in this world'; Williams followed Tennyson[7] in spelling him with a second 's'; the historic Taliesin became incorporated into Arthurian legend as the story of 'Taliesin' in Guest's *Mabinogion*.

Tristram / Nephew to Mark and lover of Iseult; 'also a great lover, but unlike Lancelot, he is out for his own hand. He is an individualist as against the State. Even his fidelity to Iseult and

---

7. 'Taliessin is our fullest throat of song,' 'The Holy Grail,' 300.

his leaving Iseult of the White Hands are largely dictated by his own ideas of what he wishes to be. His story is therefore of tragedy and death.'

Tydeg Voel / Husband of Ceridwen; his name means 'the bald.'

Virgil / Roman poet (70-19 B.C.); author of the *Aeneid*; exemplar of great poetry; also Dante's guide through hell and purgatory, in which capacity he represents the best of secular wisdom, which, however, can in itself take us no further than limbo, despite his having been considered to have foretold Christ in *Eclogue* IV.

Zemarchus / Byzantine ambassador who concluded a silk trade treaty with a Turkish khan, so not primarily a trader.

PLACES IN THE TALIESSIN POEMS: A GAZETTEER

This is intended to be comprehensive, so it includes places with no special symbolic significance, e.g. Alp, Burma, as well as those important in the symbolic geography. Only some of the places (marked with an asterisk) have a function in the organic body on the map, but there are more than the map gives.

Actium / Town in Epirus, Greece, near where Octavian (Augustus) decisively defeated Antony and Cleopatra in a sea battle, 31 B.C..

Almesbury / Convent of white nuns which Blanchefleur (Dindrane) joins and where Galahad is brought up.

Alp / One of a mountain range in Switzerland and neighbouring countries.

Apennine / Italian mountain range; St Benedict founded twelve monasteries in the hills.

Ararat / Resting place of Noah's ark; scene of first act of salvation; God's pledge to man.

Archangel / city on the White Sea in the far north.

Arimathea / Town north-west of Jerusalem (modern Ramathaim), original home of St. Joseph who begged Christ's body from Pilate and later brought the Holy Grail to Britain (*FA*, 70-2).

Athens / Greek philosophy.

Badon / Hill site of battle where Arthur decisively defeated his enemies; variously identified: Williams prefers Liddington Hill near Badbury (*FA*, 8-10).

Broceliande / 'South west of Logres; both a forest and a sea; in this sense it joins the sea of the antipodes which lies among its roots; mystically the 'making' of things.'

Burma / Country most vulnerable to invasion from P'o-l'u.

Byzantium*[8] / Capital of the (Christian) Empire; built on the Golden Horn; 'the whole concentration of body and soul rather than any special member; the Throne is the place of eternity'; 'the navel or point of union in the Empire's capital'; 'not life, nor death, but meaning'; 'the central City of the Co-inherent and Incarnate' (DD,92).

Caerleon / 'City of the Legions,' on the River Usk, where Archbishop Dubric crowned Arthur.

Camelot / Arthur's capital (identified by Malory with Winchester); 'place of the King's court and administration of man's daily life and work; the seat of life without direct revelation of joy, therefore of love in loss.'

Canterbury / See of the primate of England, though Dubric's cathedral is at Caerleon.

Cappadocia / Province of Asia Minor, named in the New Testament, later the origin of the Cappadocian Fathers, of whom St Basil the Great established the monastic rule for the church in the east.

Carbonek / Seat of King Pelles, the Wounded King; in Broceliande; 'castle of the Hallows; there are in its chapel the Grail and the Spear'; 'the seat of dedication, of the Church, of the attempt to know goodness more directly than through work or home or art, the seat of the Hallows and direct communication.'

---

8. Strictly speaking, the name Byzantium is an anachronism, as the city was called Constantinople from 330, when Constantine inaugurated his new capital, to the Turkish conquest of 1453, as Williams would have known from Gibbon. But Byzantium, as well as being 'surely one of the most magically resonant place-names in all history' (John Julius Norwich, *Byzantium*) is easier for verse, and had become established in the nineteenth century for the city and Byzantine for the later eastern empire. Williams decided to use the name Byzantium before reading Yeats's two Byzantium poems (*Image of the City*, 181).

Caspian / Inland sea east of Caucasus.

Caucasia / Mountainous region between the Black and Caspian Sea; 'buttocks; basic senses; direct sex; village society'; 'natural, uncomplicated joy and beauty, the basic manual work of the world, essential balance in the body and in all thought and life.'

Cordova / Capital of Islamic Spain.

Cornwall / Kingdom of Mark.

Danube / The river marks the northern boundary of the Roman Empire.

Egypt / Incorporated in the Empire after the battle of Actium; origin of Christian monasticism: 'The great and sacred labour in the imperial palace was balanced by the sacred and ascetic labour of the solitaries' (DD, 54).

Elburz* / Caucasian mountain (strictly the whole range) south of the Caspian Sea, whose peak is above the snow line but with forest at the foot; 'a Caucasian mountain; the grand type of the mingled lowness and height, fertility and chastity, verdure and snow of the visible body. It was also Prometheus's mountain; the bringing of fire for every purpose.'

Empire* / Christian Roman Empire with capital at Byzantium (Constantinople); 'all creation; unfallen man; a proper social order; the true physical body; the Empire is the pattern; Logres the experiment;' 'the frontier lay, uncertain and vibrating, south of the Pyrenees, along the coast of Africa, up the coast of Asia, inward around Asia Minor . . . and along the Caucasus to the Persian Sea' (DD, 92).

Gaul* / Roman province, larger than modern France and extending to the Rhine; 'fruitfulness; breasts; traditional organization; scholastic debates and doctrines; theology.'

Golden Horn* / Site of Byzantium on the Bosphorus.

India / Country next at risk from P'o-l'u after Burma.

Isle of the Sea / Britain.

Ispahan* / City of Persia (modern Esfahan); rectum; place of ejection; Moslem rejection of matter as holy; dualism; it became the Persian capital and a famous and beautiful city but not until the seventeenth century.

Jerusalem* / Capital of the Holy Land; site of Christ's passion; the genitals; 'the womb, the origin of the Christian faith.'

Jura / Mountain range and region of eastern France (Gaul).

Lateran* / Basilica of the Pope on the Coelian hill in Rome; 'the Mother and Mistress of all churches' (DD, 190).

Logres* / King Arthur's Land (Welsh *Lloegr*); Britain regarded as a province (theme) of the Empire, awaiting the coming of the Grail; 'the head, or conscious direction and intelligence.' (The poems presume that Arthur regained Britain for the Empire, cf. *FA*, 83, but moved the capital to Camelot.)

Logres-in-the-Empire / Arthurian Britain fulfilling its proper function.

Lombardy / Region of northern Italy; an independent kingdom in the sixth century A.D..

London / Provincial capital in Roman times.

London-in-Logres / Capital of Britain as Logres, so Camelot ('Taliessin in the School of the Poets' 1, and Lewis, *AT*, 197); manifestation of the City.

Lupercal* / Cave of the she-wolf who suckled Romulus and Remus, at the foot of the Palatine Hill in Rome, where the fertility festival known as Lupercalia was later celebrated (*Aeneid*, VIII. 343; Shakespeare, *Julius Caesar*, opening scenes).

Lutetia / Paris.

Marathon / Site of the decisive battle at which the Athenians defeated the Persians in 490 B.C.

Mecca* / Holiest of Moslem cities; given in the map but not mentioned in the poems.

Monsalvat / Legendary castle in Spain.

Mons Coelia* / Hill in Rome on which stands the Lateran, named from the Etruscan Cœlius Vibenna.

Monte Cassino / Monastery between Rome and Naples founded in 529 by St. Benedict whose rule has dominated Western monasticism.

Nazareth / Christ's childhood home.

Narrow Seas / English Channel (DD, 47).

Omsk / Russian city, chosen for its remoteness.

Orkney / Skull-stone, seat of Lot and Morgause.

Persia / Home of Zoroastrianism, a dualistic religion.

P'o-l'u[9] / Antipodean Byzantium, the 'opposite and infernal state'; 'Chinese name, of about the period, for the point of Java—the extreme point (nobody knew New Zealand then); the vision [of the Empire] reversed'; the desired opposite of every effort towards glory.

Portius Iccus / Slip for Portus Iccius, modern Boulogne, from where Caesar sailed for Britain (*Bell. Gall.* 5. 2 and 5). The text should be emended.

Pyrenees* / Mountain range dividing Moslem Spain from the Christian Empire.

Palatine* / The principal of the seven hills of Rome.

Rhine* / The river was the original boundary of Roman Gaul.

Rome* / Paganism; law; empire; the hands; as seat of the Pope reference is usually to Lateran.

Sarras / Island of the Trinity; also a city: 'the divine city'; 'beyond the seas of Broceliande'; everywhere by achievement and so not marked on the map.

---

9. Williams's spelling is not consistent: in *Taliessin through Logres* he gives it as P'o-lu twice and P'o-Lu once; in *The Region* it occurs five times as P'o-l'u; it is also P'o-l'u in the non-Arthurian *The House of the Octopus*; his Notes have P'o-Lu. I have listed the most commonly used form, which is also the later one. This also distinguishes Williams's use from the actual P'o-lu (*sic*), which is in Sumatra.

Sinai / Scene of the first law (the ten commandments) and promises.

Snowdon / Mountain in Wales; setting of climax of Wordsworth's *Prelude*, XIV (1850 text).

Sophia* / Justinian's great church of Hagia Sophia (Holy Wisdom) in Constantinople (Byzantium).

Tabennisi / Site of the first monastery, north of Thebes in Egypt, founded by St. Pachomius in 320 (DD, 54).

Thames / River of London.

Thebaid / Upper part of the Nile valley, named after its capital at Thebes and noted for the emergence of Christian monasticism in the third century. See Egypt.

Third Heaven / Heaven of Venus (Dante, *Paradiso*, VIII); divine love.

Thule* / Legendary island considered to mark the farthest point north.

Trebizond* / City on the Black Sea marking the boundary between Christian and Moslem Europe.

Verulam / St Alban's.

Vistula / Polish river and an important trade route.

Wales / Percivale's duchy.

Wye / River and valley in Wales where Taliessin grew up; also the location of Wordsworth's *Tintern Abbey*.

A NOTE ON THE TEXT OF THE TALIESSIN POEMS

In 'The Coming of Palomides,' Palomides describes his journey to Britain, following the route travelled earlier by Julius Caesar. Lines 30-2 read:

> I too from Portius Iccus forth
> sailing came to the Logrian land:
> there I saw an outstretched hand.

The 'Logrian land' is Logres, Arthurian Britain, but what or where is Portius Iccus? In the language of textual criticism it is a *vox nihili*, a nonsense word. There is no Latin word Portius and no place called Iccus. If Williams had looked up the place from which Julius Caesar set sail in R.G. Collingwood's *History of Roman Britain*,[1] a book we know he used,[2] he would have found it given simply as Boulogne. However, he wanted the Latin, which he could have found in Caesar's own account in *de bello Gallico*, the *Gallic War*. This names the place twice as Portus Itius.[3] Portus is the normal Latin word for port or harbour. Lewis and Short's *Latin Dictionary*, the then standard work, gives no direct translation of Itius but gives Iccius as an

---

1. R.G. Collingwood *History of Roman Britain* (Oxford: Oxford University Press, 1936.
2. Williams, *The Figure of Arthur*, 8, in Williams and Lewis, *Arthurian Torso*, (London: Oxford University Press, 1948), 95. Citations from Williams's part of this book are given as *The Figure of Arthur*; those from Lewis's part are given as *Arthurian Torso*.
3. Caesar, *de bello Gallico*, 5.2 and 5. Williams could have consulted the Loeb edition by H. J. Edwards (London: Heinemann, 1917), 234 and 238.

alternative form.[4] I think it is evident that Williams meant to write Portus Iccius. Unfortunately, neither his other reference to Caesar's expedition[5] nor the earlier version of this poem, 'Palomides' Song of the Questing Beast'[6] mentions the place.

How did this mistake arise? I conjecture that Williams looked the place up but inadvertently transposed the letter 'i' either then or when he came to write it in the poem. When it came to reading the proofs, there may have been no proofreader other than himself, as *Taliessin through Logres* was published by the Oxford University Press, for which he worked. Writers notoriously find it difficult to correct their own proofs, as they read what they expect to see rather than what is there, and they are not always reliable or consistent about details of spelling. Yeats relied heavily on a proofreader at his publisher, and there are problems in the text of Eliot's poems, although he, like Williams, worked for the company that published them.

In fact, there is other evidence of oversights by Williams in the text of the Taliessin poems. The name Blanchefleur, the standard modern rendering of Chrétien's Blancheflor, is spelled thus throughout *Taliessin through Logres* (seven instances) and also in his early *Notes on the Arthurian Myth* reprinted in *The Image of the City*. He then seemed to change his mind after he renamed her Dindrane.[7] For its one occurrence in *The Region*, which was not first published by OUP, it is Blanchfleur without the first 'e'. Similarly in the unfinished and so unrevised *Figure of Arthur*, it is Blanchfleur five times (63 and four times on 69). Similarly, he wavered between P'o-lu (two references), P'o-Lu (one reference, also his *Notes for C. S. Lewis*) in *Taliessin through Logres*, before settling on P'o-l'u (five references in *The Region*, one of them in the *Preface*, and also throughout the non-Arthurian *The House of the Octopus* of 1945). These inconsistencies are trivial in themselves but demonstrate Williams's oversights. Another is more important, indeed a crux. It concerns the name Cradlemas, which occurs three times in 'The Calling of Arthur.' In his *Notes for C. S. Lewis* (reproduced complete in Cavaliero's edition) Williams writes: 'Yes. The name was meant for Cradlement; that was a pure slip.' Lewis must have queried Cradlemas, as a departure from Malory's Cradlement (*sic*, Malory I. 14[8]). Given these oversights, it is not surprising that Williams overlooked Portius Iccus. I am more surprised that C. S. Lewis did not query it, but the place is not significant in the symbolic geography of the poems, and Lewis may also have read what he expected to see. Neither Arthurian volume was reprinted in Williams's lifetime, so he did not have the opportunity to correct the text.

---

4. Charlton T. Lewis and Charles Short, *A Latin Dictionary* (Oxford: Oxford University Press, 1879), 1008.
5. *The Figure of Arthur*, 80
6. Williams, *Arthurian Poets* ed. David Dodds (Woodbridge: Boydell, 1991), 179.
7. Lewis explains the reasons for this change in *Arthurian Torso*, 138.
8. Caxton's text as in Pollard's edition of 1911 and subsequent reprints. Texts deriving from the Winchester manuscript were not published until after Williams's death.

PATTERNS OF GLORY | 93

What is to be done? Williams's own copies of the poems or Lewis's annotated copies may turn up, or there may be references in Williams's letters which resolve these issues. Otherwise, a future textual editor will have to make some decisions. Some editors pride themselves on preserving authors' original mistakes, but I think a more constructive approach is to print, wherever possible, what the author meant, if we can be sure what it is. Williams himself frequently insisted on the importance of accuracy, for example: 'accuracy is fruitfulness—it is the first law of the spiritual life.'[9] (Readers of *Descent into Hell* will remember Wentworth and the shoulder-knots.) Taking the most trivial issue first, it would be sensible to regularize the spelling of both Blanchefleur and P'o-l'u thus, in each case to the better attested form, which in the case of Blanchefleur is also the more logical. There was a historical P'o-lu in Sumatra, a trading centre, which it is worth distinguishing from Williams's infernal place in Java by the distinction in spelling. I also believe Williams would have wanted Portius Iccus corrected. Fortunately, the correct version has the same number of syllables, and, although the stress is moved forward by one syllable, the line still scans. I therefore suggest that a critical edition should emend to Portus Iccius.

Cradlemas poses a more difficult dilemma: should it be emended to Cradlement? If Cradelment were the only version in Malory, and if this poem were the only one in which Williams used this name, the case for emendation would be strong. However, there are counter examples to both. Although Lewis must have pointed out, and Williams certainly accepted, that Malory used the form Cradelment, neither seems to have remembered that the name Cradelmas occurs two chapters earlier in Malory.[10] This is presumably the same character, though for the purpose of Williams's poems it does not matter: Malory's character is one of eleven local kings; Williams's is a decadent Roman.

Furthermore, and fortunately, Williams did use this name both earlier and later. The earlier one was in 'Taliessin's Song of Logres':

> King Cradlemas worketh his bloody rites
> in the city of Camelot at his will;[11]

The later use is in an unfinished poem of 1943-4, 'The Taking of Camelot.'[12] This contains three references to Cradlemas. These instances, together with the prominence of the name in 'The Calling of Arthur,' argue against an oversight in proofreading.

It would appear therefore that at an early stage in his preparation for the Arthurian poems Williams settled on the form Cradlemas. He may have preferred it to Cradlement because it

---

9. Williams, *The Figure of Beatrice* (London: Faber, 1943), 133.
10. *Morte Darthur* ed. Pollard I. 12: King Cradelmas.
11. *Arthurian Poets*, 167.
12. *ibid*. 283-5.

provides a contrast between the meaning of the name and the character of its owner. This is a feature both in the earlier poem and particularly in 'The Calling of Arthur,' with the implied comparison between the line 'the children die' (23) and the massacre of the innocents, commemorated as childermass in medieval times.

By the time he came to write his Notes for Lewis, Williams appears to have forgotten his justification for his preferred form of the name. He may have simply remembered or felt that he did have a reason for it, without remembering what it was. He could have added to his notes for Lewis: 'Please correct your copy.' The fact that he did not do so, together with the fact that he did in fact have a precedent in Malory, would appear to clinch the case against emendation here.

THOMAS HOWARD ON THE NOVELS

One expects the Oxford University Press to encourage interest in Charles Williams, but interestingly it is the New York Branch which has given us in the same year both Mrs Hadfield's biographical study[1] and this study of the novels by Professor Howard.[2] Indeed, Williams seems to be more widely read in the USA than in the UK: Eerdmans have reissued all the novels, and he has gained, as has Owen Barfield, from the recent critical tendency to discuss the Inklings as a group. We therefore have a new generation of readers for whom the personal magic of the man is only a vague report and who know him solely through his books.

Howard's book is addressed to readers coming to the novels for the first time. The design of his book is simple: a chapter on each novel, with an Introduction and Afterword. There is, intentionally, a great deal of repetition from chapter to chapter, since each one is intended to be self-sufficient. Howard does not say so in so many words, but the kind of reader he has in mind seems to be a college student who has been assigned one Williams novel as a set text. I do not know whether to be impressed with Howard's courage in bringing these novels to this audience or to grumble at the restrictions it imposes on him.

His book suffers from a curious defensive and apologetic tone which he falls into particularly when discussing Williams's use of occult materials in his plots. Personally, I find these fascinating and evocative, and would see no point in encouraging a reader to persist who found them repellent. Howard finds himself constantly seeking to excuse. Yet one may follow

---

1. Alice Mary Hadfield, *Charles Williams: An Exploration of his Life and Work* (Oxford: Oxford University Press, 1983).
2. Thomas H. Howard, *The novels of Charles Williams* (New York: Oxford University Press, 1983.)

C.S. Lewis, who in *The Allegory of Love*, a book Williams admired, suggests that: 'For poetry to spread its wings fully, there must be, besides the revealed religion, a marvellous that knows itself as myth.'[3] And Howard's difficulty is compounded when dealing with Williams's deliberately oblique way of drawing on Christian doctrines. Lewis elsewhere stated memorably that Williams had 'restated to my imagination the very questions to which the doctrines are answers.'[4] But Howard lacks Lewis's tact in handling these questions in a literary context, and his tone is often jarring.

He begins with a concession, taken from an introduction T. S. Eliot wrote for *All Hallows Eve*, and worth reproducing: 'What he had to say was beyond his resources, and probably beyond the resources of language, to say once for all through any one medium of expression . . . What he had to say . . . was primarily imaginative.'[5] This seems a fair contention and I count it in Howard's favour to cite it at the outset. Certainly, acknowledging flaws seems to be one of the first stages to go through in learning to love an author.

But I find Howard unsatisfactory on the question of genre. He points out that Williams does not work in the tradition of the realistic novel but gives no attention to working out what tradition he does work in and what its conventions are. Dr Cavaliero has recently drawn attention to Williams's predecessors in what he calls the occult novel, and Northrop Frye once grouped Williams with other mythopoeic writers such as Hawthorne and Melville whose work was founded on naive romance.[6] Nevertheless, when all has been said for these conventions, Williams's novels remain vulnerable. The plot and interpretation are manipulated to conform to the romance expectations, whereas the events are presented naturalistically, and a gulf can open between the two. The clearest example of this is in *Descent into Hell*, in the interpretation of the two flaws in the pageant: the slowness of the actors' diction, and a defect in a detail of the solders' costumes. Stanhope's tolerance of the first is presented as admirable; Wentworth's indifference to the second is presented as damnable. Williams justifies the distinction, but it has to be read into the narrative rather than emerging naturally from it.

The individual chapters are largely expository, but some good critical points get made. In considering *War in Heaven*, Howard usefully compares the attitudes taken by the Duke and by the Archdeacon to the Graal to the Eucharistic doctrines of their respective churches:

> Both of these churches are sacramentalist in the sense of seeing that the eternal touches time at real physical points. But the Duke, being Catholic, is stoutly attached to the vessel itself. He will

---

3. C. S. Lewis, *The Allegory of Love* (Oxford: Oxford University Press, 1936), 83.
4. C. S. Lewis, 'Williams and the Arthuriad,' 191 in Charles Williams and C. S. Lewis, *Arthurian Torso* (London: Oxford University Press), 1948.
5. T. S. Eliot, Introduction to Williams, *All Hallows Eve* (New York, Pellegrini and Cudahy), 1948.
6. Northrop Frye, *Anatomy of Criticism* (Princeton, Princeton University Press, 1957), 117.

go to any lengths to rescue the cup, whereas the Archdeacon, with his typically Anglican demurral on questions like this, is prepared to let the physical item go if that must be, so long as the Love of which it is the token still rules his own heart. This would be in keeping with the Anglican refusal to work out just how the Bread and Wine at the Eucharist may be said to be the Body and Blood of Christ, whereas the Roman Church has formularies that spell it out fairly rigorously.

However, he seems to miss the point that, in the Graal mass at the end of the book, each communicant receives from the vessel according to his expectations—an idea Williams may have derived from A. E. Waite.

There is a fine sentence about the part played by the law in *Many Dimensions*:

Law is perhaps the knotted underside of a great tapestry which, seen from above, turns out to be a pattern of such beauty and perfection that our bliss at seeing it too soon would overthrow us entirely.

Howard is weakest on *The Place of the Lion*, which is unfortunate, since this and *Many Dimensions* seem to me the finest of the earlier novels. He gets into a hopeless philosophical tangle on the relation between Platonism and Christianity and to what extent Williams suggests that the visible appearance of the Platonic principles in the novel is a legitimate possibility or a fanciful extension of that philosophy. I think the source of the confusion is that Howard accepts the two-world misinterpretation of Plato, according to which visible things are parasitic on a comparable world of similar things in a mysterious second world. In fact, Williams, like most poets, accepted the Neoplatonic interpretation that it is only the principles that are ever truly knowable. This fits very well with Christian doctrine and accounts for the technical excellence of this novel.

Howard discusses *Descent into Hell* after *All Hallows Eve*, which is perverse as it preceded it by eight years. Moreover, Mrs Hadfield cites an assurance from Williams to Eliot that the later book went on from the point at which the earlier left off[7]—surely an intention confirmed by the experience of readers. However, Howard is right as against Cavaliero in treating the phantom Adela in the earlier book as specifically a succubus and therefore objective. She is, after all, real enough for the real Adela to see and be frightened of.

Despite some incidental virtues I found this a disappointing book. It is awkwardly written, over-explicit in exposition and it shirks or fudges the difficult questions. There are also too many small inaccuracies. But one must remember that it was not written for readers of

---

7. Hadfield, *Exploration*, 228.

this journal,[8] who are avowed enthusiasts, but for beginners. They may well find it helpful. Enthusiasts will probably find more illumination in Cavaliero's single chapter given to the novels than in the whole of this book.

---

8. The Charles Williams Society Newsletter.

CHARLES WILLIAMS AS A FATHER

The story of Michael Williams as it emerges from Lindop's biography is a sad one. He was born in 1922. At the age of eight he had some kind of breakdown and afterwards was prone to depression. When he was conscripted into the RAF at the age of nineteen, he again broke down and was discharged. Later there were also outbursts of anger. He seems to have been gay, and at a time when same-sex relations were illegal. Although he worked in a bookshop for a time and even did a bit of journalism with his father's encouragement, it all petered out. He never had a career or a long-term personal relationship but continued living with his mother and from time to time needed psychiatric help. Although a worthwhile life may not command a high profile and mental illness can strike anyone, one does wonder whether Williams's behaviour as a father may have contributed to or exacerbated his son's difficulties.

Certainly, he did not get off to a good start. Lindop shows him unable to adjust to the birth of his son and making frequent negative comments, although, to be fair, he also points to a more positive attitude in some poems he wrote.[1] More ominous is that children do not seem part of his romantic theology,[2] and in 1925 he wrote to Olive Willis: 'The fatherhood of the fathers is visited upon their children and our teeth are set on edge. We can't, we daren't, be as consciously paternal . . . Anyhow, the child is bound to be unhappy.'[3] Later he wrote:

---

1. Grevel Lindop, *Charles Williams: The Third Inkling* (London: Oxford University Press, 2015), 85-9.
2. *ibid.* 112.
3. *ibid.* 120.

'keeping and educating (God help us!) a child—which is the explanation of all my books—does leave one negligent and evil in manners towards all one's friends.'[4]

However, we should remember that attitudes towards child-rearing nearly a century ago were very different from now. Most women did not work outside the home after marriage and motherhood and most men saw their role as being a provider. The idea of shared parenting alongside women having their own careers was unusual then. Nevertheless, Williams's wife went back to work as a teacher but had to stop in 1930, apparently because of stress.[5] Williams was not well paid at the Oxford University Press and earnings from his books and lecturing provided a valuable supplement. There are frequent references to the cost of school fees. Furthermore, in those days there was no National Health Service and he had to pay for medical treatment, which included Michael's bout of pneumonia.[6]

Still, he seems not only to have been a workaholic at his main job but also to have taken every opportunity to take additional work lecturing, and then to write not only his books but a good deal of literary journalism. This seems to have been not only for money, but to keep him either out of the home or preoccupied when in it. His relationship with his wife was difficult and with his son almost nonexistent. Furthermore, he was extravagant. Alice Mary Hadfield tells how 'he took students and young friends out to a continuous succession of coffees, teas, lunches and suppers. He loved taxis.' She has a story of how he took her and a colleague out to eat as much lobster as they could manage.[7] Admittedly, he spent the money on others rather than on himself, but still he spent it.

The impression one gets is that his domestic life was somewhat bleak even before the tension introduced by his unconsummated affair — if that is the right phrase — with Phyllis Jones. And if this is correct, then Michael would have grown up in an emotionally starved atmosphere which in itself could have stunted his own emotional development.

Compare what we know about Williams with what we know about T. S. Eliot. Eliot was in many ways a very private man, and there was also the tragedy of the failure of his first marriage. But there are numerous accounts of him enjoying time with friends, playing with their children, having lunch with people and in general having a social life. He seemed not often to bring people to his home, but to meet them in town. But then, as a single man of his generation he probably felt unable to entertain. In his last few years, during the time of his second marriage, he enjoyed a social life with his wife Valerie.

We have more evidence about Eliot than about Williams. But Lindop provides hardly any accounts of anyone going to Williams's home and meeting with him and his wife, and few of the two of them socializing together. I can't think that this is simply because of different

---

4. *ibid.* 212.
5. *ibid.* 166.
6. *ibid.* 273.
7. Hadfield, Alice Mary, *An Introduction to Charles Williams* (London. Robert Hale, 1959), 120.

customs at a time when each sex socialized more with the same sex. He seems to have wanted to keep different areas of his life firmly apart. He could be thrown simply by meeting someone in a setting he did not control; there is an account by Lois Lang-Sims ('Lalage') of meeting him unexpectedly on an underground train: 'Charles gave a violent start and blushed literally to the roots of his hair' and then got out at the next station.[8]

It is easy to forget that much of what is taken for granted in child-rearing now is the result of the studies of the effects of the mass evacuation of children during the second world war and was not known earlier. It was quite normal to pack children off like parcels to places without any explanation, to discipline with harsh punishments, to expect obedience without question and a good deal of deference to authority. The importance of attachment to trusted adults was not generally recognized. E. M. Forster wrote of the Englishman's 'undeveloped heart,'[9] and though he was thinking particularly of those who had been boarders at English public schools, it applied more widely.

Although Williams does not come over as a person of conspicuously narrow sympathies, he may well have had little capacity or perhaps motivation to enter the world of a child. There is a story of his wonder at Michael's interest in seeing a film,[10] an ordinary enough interest, one would have thought. At around the same time he dedicated *The Figure of Beatrice* to Michael. This was a handsome thing to do, but taking the two accounts together the message seems to be: 'Enter my world: I shall not enter yours.'

How would a growing boy experience such a father? Well, Williams counted as famous: he was well known within a certain circle and published books. But if he was also emotionally remote the boy might well have felt that nothing he could do would satisfy his father or equal his achievement, and without a good deal of affirmation he might have despaired of his own abilities. We hear nothing of any parental pride in the small successes of a child's life so perhaps there was none, at least not until Michael did some reviewing under his influence. If he picked up the tension between his parents over the issue of Phyllis or, for that matter, the many other young women in his father's entourage, he might well have felt also that marriage was not a good state. And if he read any of *The Figure of Beatrice*, he could have experienced the same revulsion that some people feel about Williams: that he was extolling a fantastic, unreal and unhealthy kind of idealization of a lost love while at the same time ignoring the real wife in front of him. He would not want to take such a man as a role model while at the same time feeling trapped by the idealized image others had of him. This would be emotionally stifling.

So one has to conclude that even if Williams was not responsible for his son's difficulties,

---

8. Lindop, 387; Lois Lang-Sims, *Letters to Lalage* (Kent, Kent State University Press, 1989), 84.
9. E. M. Forster, *Abinger Harvest* (London. Edward Arnold, 1936), 15.
10. Hadfield, Alice Mary. 1983. *Charles Williams: An Exploration of his Life and Work* (Oxford. Oxford University Press, 1983, 191 .

his personality and behaviour could well have contributed to them or at least did nothing to alleviate them.

CHARLES WILLIAMS AS A LITERARY CRITIC

Among many other things Charles Williams was a jobbing writer. In that capacity he wrote a good deal of literary criticism. There are five complete books, or rather four and a half, the last being unfinished:

Poetry at Present, 1930
The English Poetic Mind, 1932
Reason and Beauty in the Poetic Mind, 1933
The Figure of Beatrice, 1943
The Figure of Arthur (unfinished), in *Arthurian Torso*, with C. S. Lewis, 1948

There is also a large number of essays. Some of these were collected by Anne Ridler in *The Image of the City*, 1958, but many interesting ones were not, and I shall be referring to some of these.[1] There is also a number of reviews of detective stories, to which I shall not be referring. And there is editorial work of various kinds, including anthologies with introductions and notes, retellings and similar work. A particularly important contribution of this kind was his edition of the poems of Gerard Manley Hopkins.

Related to this is the editorial work he did for the Oxford University Press, which, because it is unsigned, is largely invisible to us. We know from Alice Mary Hadfield, for example, that he had a considerable part in the original *Oxford Dictionary of Quotations* (1941), and I suspect

---

1. In 2017 the present writer edited a further selection of these, *The Celian Moment and Other Essays* (Carterton: The Greystones Press).

he wrote the preface. We know that he was responsible for commissioning W. B. Yeats to compile *The Oxford Book of Modern Verse* (1936) and W. H. Auden for *The Oxford Book of Light Verse* (1938).[2] The first was a disaster and the second a success. He may have been involved in the selection of poets for the series Oxford Standard Authors, which has some surprising inclusions and omissions.[3] At the end of his life he would have liked to publish the book by Robert Graves which became *The White Goddess*.[4] In all this work he exercised critical judgement, but, as in the parallel case of his slightly younger contemporary T. S. Eliot, it is a largely unexplored field.

Before looking at the books and essays in more detail I want to begin with some general considerations about Williams as a literary critic. The first thing to say is simply that this is a considerable body of material; he actually wrote far more literary criticism than theology and of the rest of his work only the novels form a comparably important body of work. Poetry, particularly the mature Arthurian poetry, is of course another matter. But the large bulk of literary criticism compared to the small bulk of mature poetry suggests another comparison with Eliot, who also wrote far more criticism than original poetry.

And in fact, some of Williams's other books which present themselves as being about other matters, in fact contain literary criticism. The very early *Outlines of Romantic Theology*, written in 1924 but not published until 1990, contains a chapter called 'Doctors and Documents.'[5] The doctors of romantic theology turn out not to be theologians at all, at least not the kind of people one thinks of as doctors of theology, such as Anselm and Aquinas, but the poets Dante, John Donne and Coventry Patmore, together with Malory. All these people are normally thought of as literary writers, not as doctors of divinity.[6] And at the other end of his career, in *The Forgiveness of Sins*, 1942, we find a chapter on 'Forgiveness in Shakespeare' as well as his main discussion of Blake's long poem *Jerusalem*.[7]

Next, we should note the range of his literary interests. He was most seriously interested

---

2. Alice Mary Hadfield: *Charles Williams: an exploration of his life and work* (Oxford: Oxford University Press, 1983), 79, 140-1.
3. Inclusions: Alice Meynell, Williams' mentor; Robert Bridges, who was still alive and in copyright (but he was Poet Laureate); and Lascelles Abercrombie. Omissions: the Metaphysicals, apart from Donne (though Herbert was in the smaller World's Classics series), Pope. Of course, commercial considerations, the presence of rival editions or the absence of suitable editors might all have played a part in these decisions.
4. Martin Seymour-Smith, *Robert Graves: His Life and Work* (London, Hutchinson, 1982), 397-8. Cf. also Williams, *To Michal from Serge: Letters from Charles Williams to his wife, Florence, 1939-1945*, ed. Roma A. King, Jr. (London, Kent State University Press, 2002), 209.
5. Williams, *Outlines of Romantic Theology* (Michigan: Eerdmans, 1990).
6. Donne did in fact become a Doctor of Divinity but not until after he wrote the love poetry which Williams regards as embodying his teaching for this purpose.
7. Williams, *He Came Down from Heaven* and *The Forgiveness of Sins* (London: Faber, 1950), 111-8, 177-81. *The Forgiveness of Sins* first published 1942.

in poetry, which he once described in passing as 'the noblest of human activities.'[8] Next to poetry come Malory and the Arthurian romances, some of which are indeed in verse, but which I think he read in prose translations. He was not greatly interested in English poets earlier than Shakespeare, but he cared passionately about Virgil and Dante, whom he read at least to some extent in the original—another parallel to Eliot. He did occasionally write about serious prose fiction: the preface to his anthology of *Victorian Narrative Verse* begins with a discussion of the novels of George Eliot,[9] and there is a sympathetic treatment of D. H. Lawrence in his essay on 'Sensuality and substance.'[10] But it was poetry to which he constantly returned.

And we should note that his tastes in poetry were formed before the revolution that was brought about by Eliot. I need to take a moment to explain this. Eliot not only brought about a change in poetic language and subject, for which *The Waste Land*, 1922, continues to stand as the representative moment; he also helped inaugurate a new era in literary criticism. He was not alone in this. I. A. Richards was another founding father and F. R. Leavis and the *Scrutiny* group carried through a systematic programme based on their ideas. In so doing we may think they coarsened them. But the result formed the sensibility of not one but several generations of students and hence of many school and university teachers of English literature in a way that has still not wholly passed away. I should perhaps add that William Empson was a somewhat maverick outsider in this movement. They also had their American equivalents, such as Cleanth Brooks, Austin Warren and John Crowe Ransom, and it was Ransom who called the whole movement the New Criticism.[11]

The New Criticism emphasized close analysis of the texture of poetry, it valued 'a firm grasp of the actual,' poetry 'must be in relation to life, it must not be cut off from direct vulgar living'—I take these phrases from René Wellek.[12] It was part of the movement to give a much lower place to Milton and the Romantic poets than had been customary, and to elevate the Metaphysicals and the Augustans to a higher place. And though no school of criticism fails to engage with Shakespeare, both the quality and the quantity of the work produced by the *Scrutiny* group was disappointing.[13] (Eliot, Richards and Empson did, however, produce some remarkable essays on Shakespeare.) It also tended to avoid consideration of the actual subject of the written work, so as to resist moving into philosophical or historical or theological matters. This was because, as the movement got established in universities, it wanted to win

---

8. Williams, *Poetry at Present* (Oxford: Clarendon Press, 1930), 84.
9. Williams (ed.): *Victorian Narrative Verse* (Oxford: Clarendon Press, 1927), iii-v.
10. Williams, *The Image of the City and other Essays* (London: Oxford University Press, 1958), 68-75.
11. John Crowe Ransom, *The New Criticism* (Norfolk: New Directions, 1941).
12. Quoted by Leavis in *The Common Pursuit* (Harmondsworth: Penguin, 1962 (1952)), 215.
13. This is not just my view. An article by J. M. Newton, an ardent Leavis disciple, '*Scrutiny*'s failure with Shakespeare,' *The Cambridge Quarterly*, Vol.1 No. 2, 1965, greatly annoyed Leavis.

acceptance for the study of literature as an academic discipline of its own, and not as a handmaid to some other discipline.

Now Williams formed his literary tastes in an earlier age. Though he was only two years older than Eliot, it feels almost as if he were from a generation earlier. And on all the points I have mentioned he took the opposite view to that of the New Critics: he was not especially interested in close analysis though he was perfectly capable of it when he chose. He was quite happy to write impressionistically. He held to the older valuation of Milton and the Romantic poets. He engaged frequently and successfully with Shakespeare, his own experience as poet and dramatist no doubt helping him. And far from resisting moving into philosophical or historical or theological matters, his characteristic move, as I have already implied, was precisely to use poetry to illustrate spiritual truths.

Not only were his tastes different from those which have been formed under the influence of the New Criticism, but his audience was different also. Much of the contemporary audience for criticism consists of current or past professional students of literature, most of whom have been to university and many of whom are teachers. In those days far fewer young people went to university but there was a strong self-improvement movement among all strata of society, so that many people went to evening classes to study literature in an enthusiastic but non-academic way. There was a much greater emphasis on the written word anyway, and visual media such as films, television, computers and mobile phones either did not exist or occupied a much smaller part of people's lives. And people were more familiar with the Bible and had at least some knowledge of Christian doctrine; Williams frequently alludes to the Bible in the King James version and to the *Book of Common Prayer*.

Williams wrote for such people and indeed must have drawn on his own experience of teaching evening classes. His experience as an Oxford academic came much later. And he does not write like an academic or for a primarily academic audience. This can be refreshing, in that he does not employ the more cumbrous paraphernalia of scholarship. But it can also be maddening: he is quite capable of discussing a poem without quoting it or giving any clue as to where it is to be found, what its first line or title is, or where a passage comes in a play. I should say that he does usually seem to check his quotations, but his critical books could do with annotations giving proper references.

However, it would be wrong to give the impression that Williams went his own way, unaware of and uninterested in the literary discussion that was going on around him. Not only would that have been an absurd stance for someone whose day job was as a publisher, but it is demonstrably wrong, and I shall try to place him in the context of contemporary literary thought.

One final general point: I am sure that for Williams, as certainly for Eliot[14] and I expect

---

14. Eliot, *On Poetry and Poets* (London: Faber, 1957), 106.

most imaginative writers, his criticism was really a by-product of his poetic workshop. He saw himself most of all as a poet, and I think that everything he wrote was in some way intended to help him articulate and realize his poetic vision, using the older poets as teachers, companions and friends. I need give only one example: in the Preface to his anthology of Victorian Narrative Verse there is a detailed discussion of the strengths and weaknesses of Tennyson's *Idylls of the King*, poems which do not appear in the anthology itself. His conclusion is that 'The weakness of the Victorian age, as of the *Idylls*, is in its concern with conduct but its failure artistically to suggest an adequate significance in conduct.'[15] He is clearly thinking of his aims in his own projected Arthurian cycle and how he felt, as he acknowledged later, a 'vague disappointment' with Tennyson[16] which acted as a stimulus to him.

Let us turn then to his first published critical volume, *Poetry at Present*, published in 1930. The choice of poets is very much of its time: there are some names you would expect to see: Hardy, Housman, Kipling, Yeats, de la Mare, Eliot and Graves, and there are some names whose reputations have faded considerably: Bridges, W. H. Davies, Chesterton, Masefield, Ralph Hodgson, Wilfrid Gibson, Lascelles Abercrombie, the Sitwells and Edmund Blunden. You will notice that apart from Blunden there are no war poets: no Isaac Rosenberg, Wilfrid Owen or Siegfried Sassoon. Also, apart from Eliot, who was by then anyway a British citizen, there are no Americans: no Frost, Pound, or Wallace Stevens, all of whom had made reputations by 1930. All three, and others, had been considered by Robert Graves and Laura Riding in their *Survey of Modernist Poetry* of 1927, which was considerably more forward-looking than Williams's book, but this had little circulation.[17]

There is an oddity about Williams's book: each essay is followed by what he calls an End Piece, a short poem, which considers the subject of the essay in a pastiche of the writer's own style. I find most of these successful neither as poetry nor as criticism and I am surprised that the Oxford University Press was prepared to accept them. The one exception to this, to my mind, is the poem on Kipling. Here are the first two stanzas:

> Caesar stood on the ramparts
> of the farthest Roman wall,
> with the camps and marches behind him
> that meant a conquered Gaul;
> and wide before him a ghostly sea:
> saying: 'And what may Britain be?'

---

15. Williams (ed.), *Victorian Narrative Verse*, vi.
16. Williams, *The Image of the City*, 179.
17. Robert Graves with Laura Riding, *A Survey of Modernist Poetry* and *A Pamphlet against Anthologies* (Manchester: Carcanet, 2002 (*Survey* first published 1927)).

> Caesar stood on the ramparts,
> hearing how boatmen hear
> the calling ghosts at midnight
> and rise in haste and fear
> those travellers o'er the straits to row;
> saying: 'Where the ghosts go Rome may go.'[18]

You will notice here an early version of the passage on Caesar's crossing of the channel in 'The Coming of Palomides' in *Taliessin through Logres*.

But in the main discussion there are many good things. I shall pick out a few. Here is Williams on Hardy:

> One is haunted by a sense that Hardy takes inevitable moods a little too seriously, and omits the normal reaction which is so close as to make part of the mood itself. Every lover at times sees his mistress as something less than ideal, but not every one 'worries' over it quite so much. Every one at times feels that the eternal beauty he remembers and desires and adores is not quite adequately manifested in his particular young lady.[19]

He says also of Hardy:

> He has done as a poet what he could not do as a philosopher; he has made the idea convincing by his emotional statement of it and his emotional revolt against it.

And what Hardy has done—here I paraphrase—is to portray a universe without providence and almost without hope. Williams commends the stage directions rather than the verse of *The Dynasts*, and particularly this passage:

> The nether sky opens, and Europe is disclosed as a prone and emaciated figure, the Alps shaping like a backbone, and the branching mountain-chains like ribs, the peninsular plateau of Spain forming a head. Broad and lengthy lowlands stretch from the north of France across Russia like a grey-green garment hemmed by the Ural mountains and the glistening Arctic Ocean.

Here we see a germ of the idea of Europe as a body which we find later in the Taliessin poems.

Similarly perceptive I find his comment on Housman. He says:

---

18. *Poetry at Present*, 55.
19. The Hardy references are 6-7, 13 and 15.

Mr Housman, who has no concern for romantic love except as a keen and often thwarted delight, has restored the love between friends to something approaching its right place. When the two books [*A Shropshire Lad* and *Last Poems*] have been read this is left in the mind as the chief satisfaction, the most enduring peace of man.[20]

Now we all know nowadays that Housman was gay and suffered for most of his life with an unrequited love for Moses Jackson. But at the time Williams wrote his essay this was unknown, the poems in which Housman was more candid about his feelings were unpublished, and homosexual activity was a criminal offence. So it was acute for Williams to deduce from internal evidence alone that love between male friends was the key issue to Housman.

To me the most interesting essays are those on W. B. Yeats and Walter de la Mare. In both of these Williams considers how each poet uses myth and magic. He distinguishes Yeats's use from that of the Elizabethan poets:

But there is a more important difference—or more important anyhow for our purpose—between Mr. Yeats and the Elizabethans, and it is in the countries they have separately explored. A still half-fabulous world provided the earlier poets with inventions, myths, and dreams. But for us all strangeness, most adventure, and in a growing sense all space, must be found within. It is rather in ideas of the world than in the world that novelty and familiarity must lie, and it is by the recognition of the inner in the outer that most of us find satisfaction, by the accommodation of the phenomenal world to our beliefs and consistencies. How far that world is patient of our imposed interpretations—whether they be those of ancient or modern science—is another matter, and one fortunately which need not be discussed in speaking of poetry. For we are then primarily concerned not with how just any poet's myth of the universe may be, how far we may expect to be able to make our own actualities correspond with it, but only with how he sees and states it. Elements or elementals, both are credible then (and for that matter at any other time also).[21]

He goes on:

But magic and faery, and those other old alchemical wisdoms in which Mr. Yeats has found interest, what is their poetic value? It is perhaps the continual suggestion of other possibilities than the normal mind is conscious of. Since this verse does not give us (as naturally it could not) instruction how to work spells and practise the true alchemy and discover faerie kingdoms, we

---

20. ibid. 34.
21. The Yeats references are 60-1, 63, 64.

are not concerned with it as practical doctrine; it is but the effect of these continual apostrophes, invocations, and visions, to which we look.

and adds:

Nowhere is the whole purport of this desire set out more exactly than in the talk between Forgael and Aibric in *The Shadowy Waters*.

I don't think any other early reader of Yeats realized the importance of *The Shadowy Waters*. The first academic critic to have agreed seems to be Harold Bloom, who wrote: 'It is doubtful that any later poem by him [Yeats] contains as much of the whole man, or indicates the full scope of the poet's imaginative quest.'[22]

I should note also that Williams seems mainly interested in Yeats's earlier work, which he quotes in the early published versions rather in than in the revised versions which modern readers are used to. He quotes nothing from *The Tower*, which came out in 1928 and was Yeats's latest published volume at the time. This is generally, and I think rightly, considered to be Yeats's finest single volume; it contains such pieces as 'Sailing to Byzantium,' 'Leda and the Swan' and 'Among School Children,' so Williams's failure to notice its quality is a serious lapse. On the other hand he had read Yeats's book of occult wisdom *A Vision*, which had been published in its first version only in a limited edition of 600 copies, which shows that his interest in Yeats's ideas was deep.[23]

The essay on Yeats is suggestive, but the one on de la Mare seems to me even finer, in fact the best essay in the book. There is a splendid paragraph on de la Mare's treatment of death:

It is not death understood, as it is normally understood by most of us, as a state devoid of experience and empty of realization. Whatever our intellectual beliefs may be, the word death generally suggests a 'naughting' of all that we know. We may expect to know other things and even dimly hope to know lovelier; but such expectation and hope are slender emotions. In Mr. de la Mare's poems there is a state of removed ecstasy; it is as though death had become, not a gate to experience, but itself a rich experience, a summing-up and transcending of all present beauty and richness. It is removed in two senses; first, it is—as it must be in poetry—not something to be looked forward to in time and with the natural mind, but to be felt here and with the 'holy imagination' which Blake perceived to be the Saviour of men; it is therefore something more removed than a promise, being a state which exists already within us, but into which we have not entered. And secondly, it is a state which is beyond, and beyond in the sense of including,

---

22. Harold Bloom, *Yeats* (London: Oxford University Press, 1970), 133.
23. *Poetry at Present*, 5.

PATTERNS OF GLORY | 111

those other experiences of fear and mistake and terror. These, which are separate poems, are elements of the whole; transforming these into beauty, Mr. de la Mare has persuaded us of an inclusive ecstasy.[24]

And for a demonstration that Williams could do close analysis when he chose, consider his discussion of *The Song of Finis*. Here is the poem:

> At the edge of All the Ages
>   A Knight sate on his steed,
> His armour red and thin with rust,
>   His soul from sorrow freed;
> And he lifted up his visor
>   From a face of skin and bone,
> And his horse turned head and whinnied
>   As the twain stood there alone.
>
> No bird above that steep of time
>   Sang of a livelong quest;
> No wind breathed,
>   Rest:
> 'Lone for an end!' cried Knight to steed,
>   Loosed an eager rein—
> Charged with his challenge into Space:
>   And quiet did quiet remain.

Williams's comment concentrates on the last line:

'And quiet did quiet remain.' We are—to put it clumsily—*there* even to experience that quiet, and yet we are *not* there; nothing is there. The single image has vanished into space; we are, for a moment, in a state beyond images, and therefore beyond intellect. Poetry has many ways of doing this but it rarely does it so simply and finally as here.[25]

He also has a very suggestive account of what might be called mysticism:

If all theological connotation, all dogma, all ordinary piety, could be emptied out of the word religion, then this poetry might be called religious poetry. If the word mystical were not used nowadays for every cheap sensation and every indolent thought, it might almost be called mystical poetry; and if magic could ever lead to mysticism one would be tempted to say it had

---

24. The de la Mare references are 85, 89, 91.
25. Williams might also have noted the echo of Coleridge's 'The Knight's Tomb.'

done so here. In an unnatural and fascinating labour we might even attempt to arrange these poems in some order of their soft movement from state to state of that little-explored world.

You will have noticed that all these passages suggest some of Williams's own poetic aims. The essay on Masefield almost makes me want to have another look at him, and there is a fine passage on romanticism:

> The romantic mind is that which wholly abandons itself to some intense experience, and normally does not stabilize that by others. But this is the interior and greater romanticism. There exists also a lesser kind which has the trappings of that greater romance without its intensity. The decorations of death, the ornamentations of love, hide the thing itself, and sometimes hide it very beautifully. The substitution may be rich and lovely, but it is a substitution. Spenser, in *The Faerie Queene*, is full of it; the whole poem is a substitution of loveliness for intensity. And Mr. Masefield's long poems are of the same kind.[26]

But the essay on Eliot is, as he acknowledges in the preface, a failure. He cannot engage with Eliot's poetry and resorts to epigram:

> Whatever his more difficult poems mean, his simpler nearly always mean Hell pure and simple. But not in any prejudiced or invented mode. Mr. Eliot's poetic experience of life would seem to be Hell varied by intense poetry. It is also, largely, our experience. It is also, generally, our experience of Mr. Eliot's poetry.[27]

Williams's own judgement on *Poetry at Present* only a few years later was 'this pathetic effort of my immaturity.'[28] Nevertheless it went into a second edition the year after publication. It was not subsequently reprinted because in 1932 it was superseded by a successful rival. This was Leavis's *New Bearings in English Poetry*.[29] Leavis was, of course, the leader of the *Scrutiny* group. The strengths and weaknesses of his book are almost opposite to those of Williams: Leavis has a clear grip on Eliot and his discussion of *The Waste Land* is often reprinted separately. He struggles with Yeats, is impatient with de la Mare and dismissive of Bridges, whom Williams treats with great respect. He also has a chapter on Gerard Manley Hopkins as the great nineteenth century precursor of the moderns. The irony is that the edition of Hopkins Leavis relies on is the one which Williams edited in 1930, the same year as *Poetry at Present*, together with an excellent introduction which has only recently been

---

26. *Poetry at Present* 116-7.
27. *ibid.* 166 and see *Preface*, vii-viii.
28. Letter to Kenneth Sisam, 20 June 1935, quoted Hadfield, *Exploration*, 80.
29. F. R. Leavis, *New Bearings in English Poetry* (Harmondsworth: Penguin, 1963 (1932)).

reprinted—it is, I think, far more interesting than the essay on Hopkins Anne Ridler chose for *The Image of the City*.[30] Leavis, as one might expect, cites it only to disagree with it.[31] And Hopkins, in Williams's edition, became the great Victorian exemplar to poets of the thirties, but thanks to Leavis and not to Williams himself. The influential *Faber Book of Modern Verse* of 1936 begins with Hopkins.

But the root reason for the success of Leavis's book is that he argued an anti-romantic line consistently, whereas Williams could not articulate his pro-romantic line coherently enough, and it was lost among the large number of minor figures to whom he felt obliged to give respectful attention. Because of this Williams's book was forgotten, whereas Leavis's became the standard reference for the next fifty years at least and indeed has remained in print.

With this in mind I can half discern the ghost of the book Williams might have written had he been bolder. The great modern exemplar would have been Yeats rather than Eliot, and the great Victorian precursor would have been Coventry Patmore rather than Hopkins. The key American to be introduced would have been Wallace Stevens rather than Ezra Pound, and the hope for the future would have been in W. H. Auden rather than Ronald Bottrall, whose misfortune it has been to be remembered only as Leavis's hot tip.

We come now to the two books on the poetic mind, *The English Poetic Mind* of 1932 and its successor *Reason and Beauty in the Poetic Mind* of the following year.[32] The fundamental idea behind these books is to treat English poetry as if it were a single individual, articulated in diverse forms such as Shakespeare, Milton, Wordsworth and Keats, but retaining a fundamental identity beneath these forms. It is an idea quite close to Eliot's sense of tradition. You will remember that Eliot says:

> The historical sense compels a man to write not merely with his own generation in his bones, but with a feeling that the whole of the literature of Europe from Homer and within it the whole of the literature of his own country has a simultaneous existence and composes a simultaneous order. This historical sense, which is a sense of the timeless as well as of the temporal and of the timeless and of the temporal together, is what makes a writer traditional.[33]

The problem which Williams summons the resources of English poetry to solve is that of the divided consciousness, as expressed above all by Shakespeare in *Troilus and Cressida*:

---

30. It is included in *The Celian Moment and Other Essays*.
31. Leavis, *New Bearings*, 137.
32. Oxford: Clarendon Press, 1932 and 1933.
33. Eliot, 'Traditional and the Individual Talent,' *The Sacred Wood* (London, Methuen, 1950 (1920)), 49; also in *Selected Essays* (London: Faber, 1952 (1931)).

The crisis which Troilus endured is one common to all men; it is in a sense the only interior crisis worth talking about. It is that in which every nerve of the body, every consciousness of the mind, shrieks that something cannot be. Only it is.

Cressida *cannot* be playing with Diomed. But she is. The Queen *cannot* have married Claudius. But she has. Desdemona *cannot* love Cassio. But she does. Daughters *cannot* hate their father and benefactor. But they do. The British Government *cannot* have declared war on the Revolution. But it has. The whole being of the victim denies the fact; the fact outrages his whole being. This is indeed change, and it was this change with which Shakespeare's genius was concerned.

> This she? no, this is Diomed's Cressida.
> If beauty have a soul, this is not she;
> If souls guide vows, if vows be sanctimony,
> If sanctimony be the gods' delight,
> If there be rule in unity itself,
> This is not she. O madness of discourse,
> That cause sets up with and against itself;
> Bi-fold authority! where reason can revolt
> Without perdition, and loss assume all reason
> Without revolt: this is, and is not, Cressid.
> Within my soul there doth conduce a fight
> Of this strange nature, that a thing inseparate
> Divides more wider than the sky and earth;
> And yet the spacious breadth of this division
> Admits no orifice for a point as subtle
> As Ariachne's broken woof to enter.
> Instance, O instance! strong as Pluto's gates;
> Cressid is mine, tied with the bonds of heaven:
> Instance, O instance! strong as heaven itself;
> The bonds of heaven are slipp'd, dissolv'd and loos'd;
> And with another knot, five-finger-tied,
> The fractions of her faith, orts of her love,
> The fragments, scraps, the bits, and greasy reliques
> Of her o'er-eaten faith, are bound to Diomed.

Troilus sways between two worlds. His reason, without ceasing to be reason, tells him that this appearance of Cressida is not true; yet his loss is reasonable and cannot protest because this is the nature of things. Entire union and absolute division are experienced at once: heaven and the bonds of heaven are at odds. All this is in his speech, but it is also in one line. There is a world where our mothers are unsoiled and Cressida is his; there is a world where our mothers are soiled and Cressida is given to Diomed. What connexion have those two worlds?

Nothing at all, unless that this were she.

It might be too much to say that the line is the first place in which that special kind of greatness occurs in Shakespeare; but it is, I think, true to say that never before in his work had such complexity of experience been fashioned into such a full and final line. It is his power entering into a new freedom.[34]

It is worth adding at this point that Williams later devised a specific term for this predicament: he called it an Impossibility: 'something that could not be, and yet was.'[35]

It is worth comparing Williams' analysis of this passage with the later one by I. A. Richards, the founding father of the New Criticism.[36] Richards is very close to Williams—I wonder whether he had read *The English Poetic Mind*—but where Williams says: 'Entire union and absolute division are experienced at once: heaven and the bonds of heaven are at odds,' Richards says: 'When the valuations become irreconcilable and insuperable, the thing splits and the thinker (or thinger) then has to remain *one* (if he can) himself.' In other words, Williams's emphasis is on the contradictory perception, Richards's on the internal split in the perceiver.[37]

Williams goes on to suggest that in *Antony and Cleopatra* the contradiction is resolved:

The crisis of Troilus and Cressida is wholly reversed and resolved. The domination of that thing inseparate is turned back, and is dominated by the mind of man, and poetry which explores the mind of man. The world which cannot be and which is is here united with the world which is and which cannot be ... The supreme thing in that scene [the closing scene] is the consummation of the poetic mind which here manages to know those two worlds as one; discovering that knowledge by expressing it.[38]

---

34. *The English Poetic Mind*, 59-60, 61.
35. Introduction to *Letters of Evelyn Underhill* ed. Williams (London: Longmans, 1943), 15.
36. Richards, I. A.: 'Troilus and Cressida and Plato' first published 1948, collected in *Speculative Instruments* (London: Routledge, 1955.)
37. Williams has to give a point to Richards in that he did not pick up the fusion of images implied by 'Ariachne's broken woof' which combines both Arachne and Ariadne with their associated myths: 'An escape from a labyrinth containing a devouring monster, with an ensuing betrayal; a penalty for *hubris* with a horrible transformation,' *Speculative Instruments*, 210.
38. *The English Poetic Mind*, 97-8.

The rest of the book works this idea out in other poets. In *Paradise Lost* Satan embodies the contradiction in himself, as is summed up in his speech on Niphates' top at the beginning of Book IV which ends:

> So farewell, Hope, and with hope, farewell Fear;
> Farewell, Remorse; all good to me is lost;
> Evil, be thou my good; by thee at least
> Divided empire with heaven's king I hold.[39]

Williams says 'The divided empire means double consciousness within him for ever. His own self-consciousness accepts and includes that.'[40]

I have to say, however, that I find *The English Poetic Mind* a difficult book. Much of it seems at first like paraphrase, and then one comes to dense and difficult passages. The central idea, which I have just attempted to expound, is clear, but not the details. I do wonder whether this is wholly my fault. I think Williams is exploring something of great importance, on the borderland between literature and something else. The something else is sometimes theology, but as often philosophy or psychology. And I do think the fact that he lacked a philosophical education—you will remember that both Eliot and C. S. Lewis had that advantage—hampered his ability to articulate his thought. What is really needed is a clear exposition of his argument. Even Mary McDermot Shideler, in what I think is the best exposition of Williams's ideas that I know,[41] eschewed offering an account of Williams's ideas on the nature and function of poetry. So the task remains.

In the place of that I would like to make two comments. The first is that Williams's interpretation of Shakespeare is paralleled by that of the poet Ted Hughes. He also has noticed the divided consciousness, though he has a different explanation for it. But this passage might be by Williams:

Hamlet, looking at Ophelia, sees his mother in bed with his uncle and goes mad; Othello, looking at his pure wife, sees Cassio's whore, and goes mad; Macbeth, looking at the throne of Scotland, and listening to his wife, hears the witches, the three faces of Hecate, and the invitation of Hell, and goes mad; Lear, looking at Cordelia, sees Goneril and Regan and goes mad; Antony, looking at his precious queen, sees the ribaudred nag of Egypt betraying him 'to the very heart of loss' and goes—in a sense—mad; Timon, looking at his loving friends, sees the wolfpack of Athenian creditors and greedy whores and goes mad; Coriolanus, looking at his wife and

---

39. *Paradise Lost*, IV 108-111.
40. *The English Poetic* Mind, 124.
41. *The Theology of Romantic Love: A Study in the Writings of Charles Williams* (New York: Harper 1962).

mother, sees the Roman mob who want to tear him to pieces, and begins to act like a madman; Leontes, looking at his wife, sees Polixenes's whore and begins to act like a madman; Posthumous, looking at his bride, who of his 'lawful pleasure oft restrained' him, sees the one Iachimo mounted 'like a full-acorned boar' and begins to act like a madman.

Shakespearean lust, this boar of blackness, emerging to do murder, accompanied—as a rule—by various signs of a hellish apparition, and leagued with everything forbidden,

> 'Perjured, murderous, bloody, full of blame,
> Savage, extreme, rude, cruel, not to trust....'

combines with the puritan mind—a mind desensitized to the true nature of nature—and produced this strange new being: Richard III, Tarquin, Hamlet, Angelo, Othello, Macbeth—men of chaos.[42]

And Hughes's view of how the mature Shakespeare plays relate to one another is very similar to that of Williams.

The second is an encomium by the poet Geoffrey Hill. He praises Williams as a critic highly and sees *The English Poetic Mind* as his critical masterpiece. However, he also does not engage with the detailed argument but instead particularly commends Williams's aphorisms, such as:

The chief impulse of a poet is, not to communicate a thing to others, but to shape a thing, to make an immortality for its own sake.

and

Poetry has to do all its own work; in return it has all its own authority.[43]

He goes on to deplore the obscurity into which *The English Poetic Mind* fell in contrast to the warm reception given the following year to Eliot's *The Use of Poetry and the Use of Criticism*.[44] Many people have been hard on that book by Eliot, starting with its author, who called

---

42. Ted Hughes: Note to *A Choice of Shakespeare's Verse*, (ed.) (London, Faber 1971), 192-3. Note that the revised 1991 edition does not contain this essay in this form. It is, however, included in Hughes's *Winter Pollen: Occasional Essays* (London: Faber 1994) as 'The Great Theme: Notes on Shakespeare.' Hughes elaborated his thesis in *Shakespeare and the Goddess of Complete Being* (London: Faber 1992).
43. Geoffrey Hill, *Collected Critical Writings* (Oxford, Oxford University Press, 2008), 563. The aphorisms by Williams come in *The English Poetic Mind*, 5 and 167.
44. Eliot, *The Use of Poetry and the Use of Criticism* (London, Faber, 1964 (1933)).

it 'an unnecessary book' in the preface. But it is much easier reading than *The English Poetic Mind* and it contains some famous passages.

Reason and Beauty in the Poetic Mind is, however, rather easier going. Not again, for the main argument, which again eludes me, except to say that, to the extent that I understand it, the title of the book should really be *Reason, Beauty* and Power *in the Poetic Mind*, as we shall see. But it has some powerful and sustained discussions of individual writers.

I want to concentrate on two sections of the book. The first is the close analysis of Keats's 'Ode to a Nightingale.' I have said that Williams could do close analysis when he chose to, and this is a bravura example of it. Here is the analysis of the first two stanzas:

> The poem opens with six important and correlated words—'aches', 'drowsy numbness', 'hemlock', 'opiate', 'Lethe'. They discover in us a sense of our capacity for sleep and death and oblivion. Whether we are conscious of it or not two other memories of hemlock are never far from the English imagination when the word is used—the cell of Athens and the gardens of Elsinore. Socrates is near, but the elder Hamlet and the poison entering 'the porches of his ears' are perhaps nearer. The memory of them encourages the lines to take us; a sleepy death is summoned.
>
> But the next two lines, the fifth and sixth, define the sensation intellectually. It is not through envy, through a grudge at happiness which arises in a conscious unhappiness, but through an excess of happiness itself. The poet has entered into the felicity of the bird's enjoyment; hemlock and the opiate and Lethe are the details of being too happy', and that over-happiness is the awareness of a song with its own elements of detail—the light-winged Dryad, the trees, the melodious plot, the beechen green, the shadows, the song of summer, the full-throated ease. And immediately on those words the poem turns off to speak of wine. Why? Why does the thought of the beaker with beaded bubbles occur now? It is no doubt realistic enough, one might well wish for a draught of wine in those admirable circumstances, but natural logic in a great poem will have a poetic logic to support or perhaps to suggest it, and the poetic logic is here. The draught of wine corresponds to the earlier draught of hemlock; it even carries on the idea of full-throated. Indeed it is on that very word that the poem has turned. The bird's throat full of song becomes the poet's feeling the wine, and has therefore transmuted his hearing into the much closer experience of tasting. Taste is more immediate than sight or hearing, and drinking a more physically intimate thing than listening to a song. But though the change in the kind of experience suggested is deeper, we are still brought back again to the theme; only by that process, that introduction of the richer experience of wine, we are now easily introduced to new details of a similar kind to those of* the first stanza, but themselves richer. Beechen green becomes country green; melodious plot becomes dance and Provençal song and sunburnt mirth, shadows numberless become the hinted dark of the deep-delved earth, and the Dryad has become the more mature and majestic Flora. And all these things in turn prepare us for an excursion—to the

plot? or even the place of sunburnt mirth? no, but to a deeper richness of which the plot itself is but an open glade, to the forest dim. The bird's song is to fade away into *that*; the song and Keats and we are about to enter together into a grander and greater imagery.[45]

And so on for eleven pages. I think it is superb. But to understand what Williams is concerned about, compare his analysis with that of Leavis, who analyzes the same poem in his *Revaluation*, published in 1936:

> It starts Lethe-wards, with a heavy drugged movement ('drowsy', 'numb', 'dull') down to 'sunk'. The part played by the first line-division is worth noting—the difference the division makes to the phrase 'a drowsy numbness pains my sense'. In the fifth and sixth lines, with the reiterated 'happy', the direction changes, and in the next line comes the key-word, 'light-winged'. The stanza now moves buoyantly towards life, the fresh air, and the sunlight ('shadows numberless') —the thought of happy, self-sufficient vitality provides the impulse, the common medium, so to speak, in which the shift of direction takes place with such unobtrusive effectiveness, the pervasive sense of luxury, is given explicitly in the closing phrase of the stanza, 'full-throated ease'.
>
> Down the throat (now the poet's) flows, in the next stanza, the 'draught of vintage,'
>
> > Cool'd a long age in the deep-delved earth,
>
> the coolness (having banished the drowsy fever) playing voluptuously against the warmth of 'the warm South'. The sensuous luxury keeps its element of the 'light-winged': there are the 'beaded bubbles winking at the brim'. This second stanza reverses the movement of the first; until the last two lines it moves towards life and the stirring human world,
>
> > Dance and Provençal song and sunburnt mirth.
>
> But the optative 'O' changes direction, as if with the changing effect (now no longer excitation) of the wine, and the stanza ends on the desire to
>
> > leave the world unseen
> > And with thee fade away into the forest dim.[46]

Now I do not want to disparage Leavis's analysis. It comes from what I think is his best book. But see how close he keeps to the verbal sense and the texture of the poem, whereas

---

45. Williams, *Reason and Beauty in the Poetic Mind*, 63-5.
46. Leavis, *Revaluation* (Harmondsworth: Penguin, 1964 (1936)), 203.

Williams opens doors, for example to 'the cell of Athens and the gardens of Elsinore.' Leavis, that is, is keen to demonstrate that literary criticism is a valid activity in its own right, as distinct from philosophy or anything else; Williams lets the poem draw us into strange other worlds which become progressively richer. It is obviously a riskier approach than that of Leavis, and it may not be a good model for students. But it is incomparably more revealing.

The other section I want to consider is the discussion of *Paradise Lost*, which constitutes Chapter VIII, 'The Deification of Reason.' This is much longer than the discussion of Keats—about 37 pages—but fortunately Williams summarizes his argument as follows:

> Those suggestions may be summed up as follows; (i) that *Paradise Lost* is read too often only as a narrative and not sufficiently as a psychological poem; (ii) that the actual nature of the theme—which is announced to be disobedience and obedience—is not sufficiently observed, nor the nature of that obedience; (iii) that the despair of Satan and the pathos of Adam and Eve are regarded as the important achievements of Milton's imagination, whereas in fact it is the transcending of that despair and pathos which is his sublimity; (iv) that that sublimity consists—precisely as Wordsworth said it did—in an exaltation of Power, Reason, and Beauty; and in the use of his verse to express at once that Power, Reason, and Beauty, and all revolts against it with their adequate and inevitable conclusion.[47] (92)

Incidentally it is because of this passage, and others like it, that I think Williams' title should really have been *Reason, Beauty and Power in the Poetic Mind*.

In elaborating his thesis I want to pick out Williams's discussion of obedience and love. He takes a passage spoken by the angel Raphael:

> Myself and all th'angelic host that stand
> In sight of God enthron'd, our happy state
> Hold as you yours, while our obedience holds;
> On other surety none; freely we serve,
> Because we freely love, as in our will
> To love or not; in this we stand or fall. (V. 535-40)

Any one who has ever begun to envisage the nature and experience of love might, one would think, have recognized in those sublime words the poetic discovery of a simple fact of that experience. It is, surely, common knowledge that in proportion as man freely loves—*loves*—he finds himself in a state of stability. I do not say it is the only state; only that it is a mark of that particular passion, once known in the pure clarity in which it is here described. The angels are angels

---

47. The *Paradise Lost* references are *Reason and Beauty*, 92-3, 00, 106-7, 117, 114, 119, 123.

—in the narrative. But in the complex psychology of the universal poem, they are man achieving for a moment a realization of himself as free; they renew the idea of service which, once known, is by its very nature freedom. 'In this we stand or fall.' But the fall is a matter of experience, not merely of doctrine or legend.

You will notice in this not only the characteristic movement of Williams's mind from the poem to the theology he finds in it, as well as the equally characteristic echo of the collect for peace from the *Book of Common Prayer*.[48] When he applies this to the fall of Adam and Eve he says:

They had been intended, they had been created, to be in a state of lordship and service at once, of domination and of subordination. They were obedient to God and lords of the world beside. But now, drunk with desire—they can hardly stop eating—they are first triumphant and indulgent, in a coarse imitation of serene mastery, and then gloomy and fearful, in a coarse imitation of serene obedience.

He goes on to explain:

Love is a matter of the intellect and the will; sensation of beatitude is (at least in man's unfallen state: it seems somehow to be different now) a result of this.

Next I want to consider Williams's discussion of Milton's portrayal of God. This has also been controversial. Williams is quite clear that:

The God of *Paradise Lost* . . . does not exist outside *Paradise Lost* any more than Macbeth exists outside *Macbeth*.

This is a subtle move; indeed, it is one C. S. Lewis seems to have forgotten when he wrote: 'Many of those who say they dislike Milton's God only mean that they dislike God.'[49] A more typical academic approach would to be separate Milton's God from any concept the critic might have of God outside the poem. Williams, however, goes on to explore Milton's literary problem in theological terms:

---

48. 'our eternal life, whose service is perfect freedom.' The idea goes back to patristic times.
49. C. S. Lewis, *A Preface to Paradise Lost* (London: Oxford University Press, 1960 (1942)), 130. I realize I am simplifying Lewis's position.

It must be admitted that Milton is struggling with a problem which even his genius could hardly solve. He had to express Omnipotence and Omniscience; he had to set that of which they were qualities into relation with created beings; and he had to turn the whole thing into a dramatic narrative. It is very difficult to put Omnipotence and Omniscience into a story, because the proportions of the story are immediately destroyed. In another sense than Cleopatra's, 'the odds is gone.' It is still more difficult to make them dramatic; which is why, if Christianity were not true, it would have been necessary, for the sake of letters, to invent it. It is the only safe means by which poetry can compose the heavens, without leaving earth entirely out of the picture. The Incarnation, had it not been necessary to man's redemption, would have been necessary to his art; the rituals of the Church have omitted that important fact from their paeans.

Following God there is heaven, which he reminds us 'is not a place but a state' and Williams goes on to expound its qualities, summing them up by saying it is 'a state of Power and Reason and Beauty' which phrase supports my view that the title should really have been expanded.

With that I want to leave *Reason and Beauty in the Poetic Mind*. The three books we have considered were written in the comparatively short period of four years and I think Williams must have felt he had written enough critical books because he did not write another one for another ten years.[50] However, he continued to write critical essays, usually as book reviews. I want to single out three of these, two of which, as it happens, have only recently been collected.

The first is his Introduction to *The New Book of English Verse*, published in 1935.[51] This has now been reprinted with the title 'The Celian Moment.'[52] Celia was, of course the name he gave Phyllis Jones, his second love, and we can feel the *frisson* with which he used this name with its private associations for what he offers as a literary device, and in a book in which he acknowledged his wife's help:

> The Celian moment (so to call it) had a double vocation—as love and as poetry—and retains for us a passion in both. It is the moment which contains, almost equally, the actual and the potential; it is perfect within its own limitations of subject or method, and its perfection relates it to greater things.[53]

However, Williams expresses himself too cryptically to be clear. His definition is derived

---

50. He did, however, consider collecting some of his essays under the title *The Celian Moment*, but this was not supported by the OUP. The present writer edited a collection of them under this title in 2017.
51. Williams (ed.), *The New Book of English Verse* (London, Gollancz, 1935).
52. It is the title essay in *The Celian Moment and Other Essays*.
53. Williams, *New Book*, 13; *The Celian Moment*, 20.

from Coleridge,[54] and it will attain its fullest exposition on the first page of *The Figure of Beatrice* some years later.

The second essay I want to consider also has a connection with Celia. In 1933 OUP issued a collection of twentieth-century English Critical Essays with an introduction which is credited to Phyllis Jones.[55] I am pretty sure this is actually by Williams: the style and the ideas are characteristic of him, and nothing we know of Phyllis Jones suggests that she could have written it herself. It has recently been reattributed to Williams and reprinted with the title 'The Office of Criticism.'[56] In it he carries further his treatment of literature as a kind of secondary revelation. He does this first in a parenthesis:[57]

> It has been thought convenient here to except in all cases man's relation to God, which may or may not be so very different from his relation to Letters, more particularly to poetry, save that for Letters some native inborn desire may or may not exist, but for the former we must believe that a native inborn desire does exist.

At the end of the essay he gives his clearest account of the function of poetry, apart from religion:

> there is nothing in this life which more arouses in our souls a knowledge of their origin and their nature than the contemplation of poetry. We know things first of all in life and we know them again more fully and more clearly in poetry: in poetry it is possible to know even pain and desolation—our own pain and desolation—as fruitful rather than sterile things.

I think Williams is here very far from the New Critics and much closer to someone like Jacques Maritain, whose book *Art and Scholasticism* was much discussed in the 1930s. I take one sentence from this: 'Artistic creation does not copy God's creation, it continues it.'[58]

The third of Williams's essays I want to mention is the introduction to the 1940 edition of Milton in the World's Classics series and reprinted in *The Image of the City*. This is one of the few critical essays that has stayed in general literary circulation, and that is for two reasons. One is that it was extravagantly praised by C. S. Lewis, in the introduction to his own 1942 book *A Preface to Paradise Lost*, which is dedicated to Williams. He said that it was 'the

---

54. *The Statesman's Manual*, 1816, 36-7; cited from John Beer, *Coleridge the Visionary* (London: Chatto, 1959), 138. also in Coleridge, *Collected Works*, Vol VI, *Lay Sermons* (Princeton: Princeton University Press, 1972), 30.
55. Jones, Phyllis M. (ed.), *English Critical Essays First Series* (London, Oxford University Press, 1933).
56. It is the first essay in *The Celian Moment and Other Essays*.
57. *English Critical Essays*, Introduction ix, xii-xiii; *The Celian Moment*, 5, 8.
58. Maritain, *Art and Scholasticism* and *The Frontiers of Poetry*, translated Joseph W. Evans, (London: University of Notre Dame Press, 1974), 60. (The first edition of the French original was published in 1920 and the first English translation in 1923.)

recovery of a true critical tradition after more than a hundred years of laborious misunderstanding.'[59] The other is that it is an important document in the Milton controversy which raged across the middle years of the last century. If you want to understand Williams's place in that controversy, I refer you to Christopher Ricks's book *Milton's Grand Style* which summed up and ended the controversy.[60] But our concern is to identify what it is about Williams's essay that so impressed Lewis.

Williams starts from the fact that Milton's reputation has been attacked, which he considers fortunate. He says:[61]

> The orthodox Chairs of Literature, it must be admitted, had for long professed the traditional view of an august, solemn, proud and (on the whole) unintelligent and uninteresting Milton.

When they found that what they had been saying for centuries with admiration was now said with contempt they found themselves helpless. But, Williams points out, there was another possibility:

> it may be put very briefly by saying that Milton was not a fool. The peculiar ignorance of Christian doctrine which distinguished most of the academic Chairs and of the unacademic journalists who had been hymning Milton had not prevented them from arguing about the subtle theological point of the Nature of the Divine Son in *Paradise Lost*. The peculiar opposition to high speculations on the nature of chastity felt in both academic and unacademic circles had prevented any serious appreciation of that great miracle of the transmutation of the flesh proposed in *Comus*. And the peculiar ignorance of morals also felt everywhere had enabled both circles to assume that Milton might be proud and that yet he might not at the same time believe that pride was wrong and foolish. It was never thought that, if he sinned, he might repent, and that his repentance might be written as high in his poetry as, after another manner, Dante's in his. Finally, it was not supposed, in either of those circles, that Satan could be supposed to be Satan, and therefore a tempter; that Christ (in *Paradise Regained*) could be supposed to hold human culture a poor thing in comparison with the salvation of the soul; or that Samson, in the last great poem, could in fact reach a point of humility at which he could bring himself occasionally to protest like Job against the apparent dealings of God with the soul.

So what Williams did was to propose that the issues the poems dealt with were real issues, and that Milton engaged with them on the territory which is at once literary, psychological

---

59. Lewis, *A Preface to Paradise Lost*, v-vi. The following references are in 26-32.
60. Christopher Ricks, *Milton's Grand Style* (Oxford: Clarendon Press, 1978 (1963)).
61. References are to *The Image of the City*.

and theological. He also made it clear that obedience in *Paradise Lost* means 'the law of self-abnegation in love,' that Satan's self-love has landed him in hell, and 'Hell is always inaccurate' and that Milton handles the very rare and difficult issue of showing the moment of choice, not only with Satan and Eve but also earlier in *Comus* and later in *Samson Agonistes*. (He does not discuss *Paradise Regained* in detail.) He also points to the delicacy and sensitivity that Milton can use and says: 'It is no doubt as a result of the long tradition of the organ-music of Milton that the shyness of some of his verse passes unnoticed.'

So this essay has generally been taken to be a considerable contribution to the debate about the nature of Milton's achievement. If Lewis is considered a somewhat partisan supporter, I should like to mention Eliot, who singled out this essay for 'the author's warmth of feeling and his success in communicating it to the reader.'[62] An opposing view is offered by Leavis, who followed up Eliot's commendation and says:

> Having taken the tip and looked at it I am obliged to report that I found it the merest attitudinizing and gesturing of a man who had nothing critically relevant to say.[63]

Before coming to *The Figure of Beatrice* I want to deal briefly with *The Figure of Arthur*. It would have been a popular introduction to the Arthurian romances. Its value in that capacity is hampered by the fact that it is unfinished, and also that I think Williams appears not to have read, and may not have been able to read, the French sources in the original and so was reliant on translations and handbooks. As a popular introduction it has in any case long been superseded.[64] However, its value to us is that it shows the way Williams, as a creative writer, rather than as a critic, thought about the Arthurian romances and their actual and potential meaning. This is both of great value in itself and also an illumination on his own actual and proposed Arthurian poems, though one should remember that the poems we have were written first. But it does not really count as a work of literary criticism.

On coming to *The Figure of Beatrice* from reading the earlier criticism the first thing to strike one is the clarification in style. What was previously somewhat misty has come sharply into focus. There is nothing tentative; Williams's enthusiasm for his author is, if anything, greater than before and more boldly expressed. The traces of archness and whimsicality in some of the earlier work have gone and been replaced by both a greater tenderness and a

---

62. Eliot: 'Milton II,' in *On Poetry and Poets*. This lecture was originally delivered in 1947.
63. F. R. Leavis, *The Common Pursuit* (Harmondsworth: Penguin, 1962 (1952)), 253. Williams makes an equally uncomplimentary reference to Leavis, though without naming him, in his essay, *The Image of the City*, 27.
64. Richard Cavendish, *King Arthur and the Grail* (London: Weidenfeld and Nicolson, 1978) represents the kind of popular account which Williams seems to have intended. Alan Lupack: *The Oxford Guide to Arthurian Literature and Legend* (Oxford: Oxford University Press, 2005) is more recent, more comprehensive, and also includes a discussion of Williams.

greater severity. The epigrams are no longer, as they sometimes were, merely verbal, but snap and bite and sting. Here are some of them:[65]

> Hell is the cessation of work and the leaving of the images to be, without any function, merely themselves. (40)
>
> The alternative to being with Love at the centre of the circle is to disorder the circumference for our own purposes. (48)
>
> Poetry cannot possess charity; it cannot be humble. It is therefore justly presented in Virgil, who precisely lacked baptism. (111)
>
> At the Francescan moment the delay and the deceit have only begun; therefore their punishment—say, their choice—has in it all the good they chose as well as all the evil. (119)
>
> The Beatrician moment is a moment of revelation and communicated conversion by means of a girl. (123)
>
> The office and function is always to be honoured; much more those from whose functions we ourselves have lived and learnt to live; much more those whom we loved. (131)
>
> Accuracy is fruitfulness—it is the first law of the spiritual life. (133)
>
> The supreme achievement of hell is to make interchange impossible. (138)
>
> Beatrice is an illumination by grace, but one could do without Beatrice; one cannot do without the City. (141)
>
> The passage of Purgatory is a passage to justice; in sin the universe is always unfair. (148)
>
> Beatrice, laughing and happy, is truth experienced in all ways. (153)

Nevertheless, when I started on this reading of *The Figure of Beatrice*, I found myself wondering whether it was a work of literary criticism at all. A good deal of it is, rather, an exposition of the Way of Affirmation of Images—Williams's fullest and clearest such exposition—illustrated from the work of Dante. This is partly because he does not shirk exposition and paraphrase, but also because, unlike most critics, far from eschewing the theological implications of the work, he embraces them. In this way it is perhaps a riposte to Eliot, who in his book on Dante, first published in 1929, had said:

> My point is that you cannot afford to *ignore* Dante's philosophical and theological beliefs, or to skip the passages which express them most clearly; but that on the other hand you are not called upon to believe them yourself.[66]

Williams, on the other hand, thought that in his beliefs what Dante thought was both

---

65. References are to *The Figure of Beatrice* (London: Faber, 1943).
66. Eliot, 'Dante' in *Selected Essays*, 257.

important and true. Indeed, his reaction on first reading Dante, as he later told Dorothy Sayers, was to say, 'But this is *true*.'[67]

In fact, Williams's book took its place in a debate that was going on at the time that considered the nature of love in medieval literature and its influence on later Western culture. A full discussion of this would be another paper, if not a book, so I shall just briefly indicate the nature of the debate. It began with the Swedish Lutheran theologian Anders Nygren's *Agape and Eros*.[68] This is a famous and influential book and Williams must have known of it, though I am not aware of any evidence that he had read it. Nygren begins with a hard distinction between Eros, by which he means the human love for the divine, classically expressed by Plato, and the love which is a response of gratitude for the love of God, which is extolled in the New Testament and which he calls Agape. He found a synthesis of the two in what he calls *caritas* religion, which was developed by Augustine and expressed by Dante, in which the Eros trait of an upward tendency is completed with love regarded as a gift of Divine grace.[69] But Nygren does not so much as mention Beatrice, so Williams might well have felt stirred to assert her importance.

Next came Lewis's *The Allegory of Love* of 1936, which promoted a view of courtly love that was widely influential.[70] Lewis considered that the appearance of romantic love in the poetry of the troubadours at the end of the eleventh century represented a real change in human sentiment and that its marks were humility, courtesy, adultery and the religion of love. Courtly love, in Lewis's reconstruction, becomes a substitute or alternative religion. As is well known, Williams wrote to Lewis praising his book, saying: 'I regard your book as practically the only one I have ever come across, since Dante, that shows the slightest understanding of what this very peculiar identity of love and religion means.'[71]

In 1938 John Burnaby's *Amor Dei: A Study of the Religion of St Augustine* included a robust rebuttal of Nygren and a different exposition of *caritas* in Augustine. He sees the dominant theme in Augustine's conception of Christian love as *desiderium*—the 'unsatisfied longing of the homesick heart,' which 'corresponds to his view of the relation of this world to the next, of Christian life as a pilgrimage, and of happiness as something impossible of realisation in

---

67. Dorothy L. Sayers, *The Poetry of Search and the Poetry of Statement* (London, Gollancz, 1963), 73.
68. Swedish original 1930. The English translation came out in instalments between 1932 and 1939, with a complete edition not appearing until 1953: *Agape and Eros* translated Philip S. Watson (London, SPCK, 1982 (1953)).
69. Nygren, *Agape and Eros*, 619-20.
70. C. S. Lewis, *The Allegory of Love* (Oxford: Oxford University Press, 1936). As is the way with scholarly fashions, it has now been called into question: Helen Cooper, *The English Romance in Time* (Oxford: Oxford University Press, 2004), 439, describes Lewis's view as 'seductive and profoundly misguided.'
71. Williams: letter to Lewis, 12 March 1936, given in Roger Lancelyn Green and Walter Hooper, *C. S. Lewis: A Biography*, fully revised and expanded edition (London: HarperCollins, 2002 (1974)), 137.

this life.'[72] Augustine's understanding of the love of God is not the 'love wherewith God loves us, but that by which He makes us His lovers.'[73]

Next came Denis de Rougemont's *Passion and Society* (French original 1939, English translation 1940),[74] which promoted a view of passionate love as one that 'looks forward to suffering, a death-desire, "the active passion of Night."'[75] I am quoting here from Williams's sympathetically written but very critical review, in which he goes on to say:

> The great tradition of romantic love—renewed like the phoenix in every generation—is quite other than the desire of death. The passion-myth is a heresy of it: at moments a temptation; in moments of agony a very great temptation. The grand pattern of the real glory takes long to explore, and involves many opposite experiences, including boredom. It too, as in Dante, leads to politics and the City.[76]

This is practically a statement of the central concern of *The Figure of Beatrice*, so I think that de Rougemont's book was also a stimulus to Williams. The year after writing his review he published the pamphlet *Religion and Love in Dante*, with the main book following two years later.[77]

I should add here that the English edition of *Passion and Society* was published by Faber, presumably on Eliot's initiative,[78] and Eliot was to go on to publish not only *The Figure of Beatrice* in 1943 but also Martin D'Arcy's *The Mind and Heart of Love* in 1945, which effectively brought this debate, or at least this episode of it, to an end.

What was Williams's contribution to this debate? Could courtly love be in any way reconciled with Christian love? The core of Williams's resolution of this lies in his understanding of the significance of Dante's apprehension of Beatrice as first expressed in the *Vita Nuova* and in particular in the canzone 'Donne ch'avete intelletto d'amore' ('Ladies that have intelligence in love'). Williams says about this:

> What Dante sees is the glory of Beatrice as she is 'in heaven'—that is, as God chose her, unfallen, original; or (if better) redeemed; but at least, either way, celestial. What he sees is something real. It is not 'realer' than the actual Beatrice who, no doubt, had many serious faults, but it is as real.

---

72. Burnaby, *Amor Dei, Amor Dei: A Study of the Religion of St Augustine* (London: Canterbury Press, 1938), 96, 98.
73. Augustine: *De Spiritu et Littera* 56, cit. Burnaby, 99.
74. Denis de Rougemont, *Passion and Society* translated Montgomery Belgion (French original 1939, English translation 1940), second edition (London: Faber 1956).
75. De Rougemont's actual phrase is '*the active passion of Darkness*,' *Passion and Society*, 46.
76. *The Image of the City*, 161. Note the echo of Eliot from the book which was so much more warmly received than *The English Poetic Mind*, *The Use of Poetry and the Use of Criticism*, 106: 'the boredom, and the horror, and the glory.'
77. *Religion and Love in Dante* (London, Dacre Press n.d. [1941]); reprinted in *The Celian Moment and Other Essays*.
78. The translator was Montgomery Belgion, who was a frequent collaborator with Eliot.

Both Beatrices are aspects of the one Beatrice. The revealed virtues are real; so is the celestial beauty.[79]

He goes on:

Such a perfection is implicit in every human being, and (had we eyes to see) would be explicit there. The Christian religion declares as much. It is certain that many lovers have seen many ladies as Dante saw Beatrice. Dante's great gift to us was not the vision but the ratification, by his style, of the validity of the vision. Where we ignorantly worship, there he defined.[80]

To love is to love and serve the function for which the loved being was created, whatever that may mean or involve; this is the definition of the Way.

The rest of the book, as indeed of Dante's life and work, can be seen as the working out of the consequences of accepting this vision as a true vision, that is, as a revelation. If you do not accept this as at least possible, or if you do not accept Williams's interpretation, then the book is not going to mean much to you; Foster and Boyde, for example, in their commentary on this canzone say sternly:

Dante is still far from being the fairly careful theologian he later became. He is a young poet working rather insecurely on the borderlines between orthodox Christianity and the 'religion' of courtly love.[81]

However, if you do follow Williams, then *The Figure of Beatrice* becomes, as Williams intended, a guide to the Affirmative Way, and the best exposition of his Romantic Theology. It is one of those commentaries which is itself an original contribution, such as, to take examples Williams would have known, John Livingston Lowes' study of Coleridge's sources, *The Road to Xanadu*,[82] or Karl Barth's commentary *The Epistle to the Romans*.[83]

But our concern is with literary criticism, and indeed there is a good deal of literary criticism in *The Figure of Beatrice*. I shall take three examples showing different kinds of approach.

---

79. *The Figure of Beatrice*, 27. With this cf. Orsino: 'Here comes the Countess; now heaven walks on earth,' *Twelfth Night*, V.1.91. The following references are *Figure of Beatrice*, 47-8, 51.
80. Note the echo of Acts 17: 23: 'Whom therefore ye ignorantly worship, him declare I unto you.'
81. Kenelm Foster and Patrick Boyde: *Dante's Lyric Poetry* (Oxford: Clarendon Press, 1967, 2 vols.), II, 100. I should, however, add that Foster's developed view was that Dante's poetry was 'so complete an expression of a trans-sexual idea of love.' The essay from which this is taken is much closer to Williams: Foster, 'Dante and Eros,' in *The Two Dantes and other studies* (Cambridge: Cambridge University Press, 1977), 37.
82. John Livingston Lowes, *The Road to Xanadu* (London: Constable, 1927).
83. Karl Barth, *The Epistle to the Romans*, trans. Edwyn C. Hoskyns (Oxford: Oxford University Press, 1933 (German original 1919)).

Firstly, consider his account of the dark wood at the opening of the *Inferno*:

> The image of a wood has appeared often enough in English verse. It has indeed appeared so often that it has gathered a good deal of verse into itself; so that it has become a great forest where, with long leagues of changing green between them, strange episodes of high poetry have place. Thus in one part there are the lovers of a midsummer night, or by day a duke and his followers, and in another men behind branches so that the wood seems moving, and in another a girl separated from her two lordly young brothers, and in another a poet listening to a nightingale but rather dreaming richly of the grand art than there exploring it, and there are other inhabitants, belonging even more closely to the wood, dryads, fairies, an enchanter's rout. The forest itself has different names in different tongues—Westermain, Arden, Birnam, Broceliande; and in places there are separate trees named, such as that on the outskirts against which a young Northern poet saw a spectral wanderer leaning, or, in the unexplored centre of which only rumours reach even poetry, Igdrasil of one myth, or the Trees of Knowledge and Life of another. So that indeed the whole earth seems to become this one enormous forest, and our longest and most stable civilizations are only clearings in the midst of it.[84]

This is an exposition of the *topos* or archetype of the forest, a fine early example of myth-criticism, a passage that might have strayed out of the pages of Maud Bodkin or Northrop Frye.[85]

Then let us take the issue of Virgil's exclusion from heaven, which has always been controversial. This is a matter which Williams had already treated, in the poem 'Taliessin on the death of Virgil' in *Taliessin through Logres*. This is his discussion in sober prose:

> This is a convenient place to say something of the recurrent question of Virgil being shut out of heaven. It must, I think, be admitted that that exclusion does, to our differently thinking minds, a little jar—in spite of our Lord's comment on St. John the Precursor. We are intensely conscious of the personal Virgil. It should however be recognized that, so far from Dante being compelled against his poetic will to keep Virgil theologically out of heaven, Dante as a poet simply could not afford to let him in. The poetry is not in the least reluctantly acceding to a theological doctrine; it is taking every advantage of the doctrine; in a sense, we may say that, if the doctrine had not been there for Dante, then Dante would have had to invent it. To think otherwise is to

---

84. *The Figure of Beatrice*, 107.
85. Maud Bodkin, *Archetypal Patterns in Poetry: Psychological Studies of Imagination* (London: Oxford University Press, 1934), Northrop Frye, *Anatomy of Criticism* (Princeton: Princeton University Press, 1957). In fact a closer parallel is Chapter Two, 'Fabulous Forests,' in Alexander Porteous, *The Forest in Folklore and Mythology* (New York: Dover, 2002 (first published as *Forest Folklore, Mythology and Romance*, 1928)). However, Porteous does not mention any Shakespearean connections and I think Williams wrote independently.

miss the real point of Virgil. The figure of Beatrice alone is enough to show that Dante set no limit to the great orderly development of natural things; the eyes of Beatrice are always human. But as there is an infinite development, so there must also be an infinite division. 'This also is thou, neither is this Thou.' Neither the Affirmations nor the Rejections are allowed to forget either half of that maxim. Virgil, the image of so much, is also the image of the necessary separation—or at least willingness towards separation—from the dearest thing. The consciousness of the sighs which trouble the air of Limbo is the consciousness of our sighs when we are expected to abandon all—for ever; and what seems to us the terrible phrase of Beatrice when she says to Virgil himself 'I am made such that your misery does not touch me' (II, 92) means a division which has to be endured. But this necessary Rejection must here be justified in its particulars. Virgil is poetry, and the greatest of European poets knew the limitation of poetry. Poetry may be as 'spiritual' as its rash devotees are in the habit of calling it. In so far as it is 'spiritual' it is of the nature of those visions and locutions from which the wise are warned to be detached. Poetry cannot possess charity; it cannot be humble. It is therefore justly presented in Virgil, who precisely lacked baptism; that is, by the theological decision of the time, the capacity for infinite charity and infinite humility. So of Virgil as philosophy, and Virgil as human learning; nay, of Virgil as the Institution itself. It is a part of the poem that Virgil should lack grace; did he not, he would be too like Beatrice herself. The *Aeneid* has *pietas* and not *caritas;* so must its author have here.[86]

This characteristically shows Williams seeing the character Virgil as primarily there to serve a function and not the other way round. This is one example of the principle Williams takes from Dante's *Monarchia*, which he also uses as the epigraph to *Taliessin through Logres*. In his translation it reads:

The proper operation (working or function) is not in existence for the sake of the being, but the being for the sake of the operation.[87]

My final example is one in which Williams demonstrates his skill in verbal analysis. This is of a passage in *Paradiso*. Dante is perplexed how, if the crucifixion was just vengeance on human sin, how could it be justly avenged. Beatrice says:

Secondo mio infallibile avviso,
come giusta vendetta giustamente
vengiata fosse, t'ha in pensier miso— (VII. 19-21).

---
86. *ibid.* 111-2.
87. *ibid.* 40.

Here is Williams's translation and discussion:

'According to my infallible advisement, how a just vendetta is justly avenged, hath sent thee into thought.' The first line is the test. Most of the English translations load Beatrice's voice with some such phrase as `according to my unerring intelligence.' On the other hand, they make her say it (since Dante did) 'with such a smile as would make a man happy though in the fire.' It follows that, if she is to show such a rich and happy delight while she speaks, it must be vital in the words; she must be enjoying them and what they mean. So, of course, she is; she is enjoying —she is amused and delighted at—this astonishing fact of her infallible knowledge. This delight the reader in general misses, so that for him she is merely portentous. But she is not portentous, any more than the alliterations and verbal variations in the other lines are portentous. She and they are joyous. God has settled it like this; it is not her doing; ascribed to the only Omnipotence be all the glory. She is not 'putting it over' Dante, or only as much as any happy femininity would, in those celestial conditions, put it over a less quick masculinity. This union of laughter and knowledge, modesty and magnificence, humility and infallibility, may be difficult to imagine. The alternative is a cultured female psychiatrist, with an officially spiritual smile. It will not serve. Beatrice is saying—any lover to any lover—'I know what you are thinking,' only (transhumanized) she is right. The phrase is imparadised by joy; we have to learn the joy by the phrase.[88]

Where there is so much to admire, it seems churlish to find fault. However, I do have a reservation: I do not think that the comparison Williams intermittently uses between Dante and Wordsworth, and specifically *The Prelude*, achieves what he wants it to. I understand that he wanted the nearest thing to an English equivalent for poetry-loving readers who wanted to have something more familiar they could compare Dante with. The trouble is that whenever he quotes Wordsworth in this book it seems a distraction rather than an illumination, and I find myself hurrying on to get back to the main argument, something I do not want to do when I read Wordsworth for his own sake. But who else could Williams have chosen? Milton would not do, because the comparison then becomes a competition and one which Milton loses.[89] If Shelley had lived, *The Triumph of Life* might have provided a suitable comparison, but it is unfinished.[90] The only romantic poet other than Wordsworth who lived long enough and continued writing visionary works was Blake, and Blake's longer poems are

---

88. *ibid.* 201.
89. There is, however, a charming passage where Williams translates a line of Dante by a line of Milton: *Figure of Beatrice*, 110.
90. Both Eliot and Lewis had drawn attention to Shelley's Dantesque qualities, particularly in this poem. See T. S. Eliot: *Selected Essays*, 264 and C. S. Lewis, 'Shelley, Dryden and Mr Eliot,' first published 1939 and so available to Williams, collected in *Selected Literary Essays* (Cambridge: Cambridge University Press, 1969); Eliot later gave a fuller encomium in 'What Dante means to me,' a 1950 lecture collected in *To Criticize the Critic* (London: Faber, 1965).

much more obscure than Dante. On the other hand, Williams did not live to write his projected book on Wordsworth, *The Figure of Power*,[91] so these passages are perhaps valuable in giving us an idea of what that might have been like.

What then do we make of *The Figure of Beatrice*? Alice Mary Hadfield says, 'For many readers it is Charles's greatest work' or at least 'the greatest of his prose works.'[92] Glen Cavaliero is more measured: after pointing out the book's dual nature as both expository and theological he says:

> This dual nature is typical of Williams's approach, but, while it accounts for the book's enthusiasm and insight, it renders it at times didactic and oracular. Although he deprecates the fault, the author appears to be rewriting his subject's work, and the result is a feeling of imaginative oppression.[93]

But the greatest influence the book has had was on Dorothy L. Sayers. She read it, as she records, 'not because it was about Dante, but because it was by Charles Williams,'[94] and it started her on her engagement with Dante which led her to produce her translation for the Penguin Classics series as well as a number of essays. On the other hand, the book has not been taken on by professional Dantists; even Barbara Reynolds, who completed Sayers's Dante translation, did not mention it in her own study.[95]

I should say at this point that I am unable to consider this book objectively. I came to it through reading Dante in Dorothy Sayers' translation and, as a consequence, I am quite unable to regard it simply as an interpretation of Dante since I see it rather as the last word of truth on much of what Williams considers. This is not to say that it is without minor and incidental flaws, but these disappear in the light of the radiance of the book as a whole.

In Canto XXV of the *Paradiso* Dante refers to his poem as a 'poema sacro,' a sacred poem, and it has been suggested[96] that he invited his readers to see it as a work equivalent to scripture in its authority. This suggestion does not come from Williams, but it is completely in keeping with the way that he thought, not only about Dante, but about all poetry: it was for him a secondary revelation, whose authority was no different and ultimately no less than that of scripture. Whether this takes too low a view of revelation, too high a view of poetic

---

91. See Ridler in *Image of the City*, 197.
92. Hadfield: *Exploration*, 211.
93. Glen Cavaliero, *Charles Williams: Poet of Theology* (London: Macmillan, 1983), 151-2.
94. Dorothy L. Sayers: "... And telling you a story ..." in *Further Papers on Dante* (London, Methuen, 1957), 1. See also Barbara Reynolds, *The Passionate Intellect: Dorothy L. Sayers' encounter with Dante* (Kent, Kent State University Press, 1989).
95. *Dante: the Poet, the Political Thinker, the Man* (London: I. B. Tauris, 2006).
96. Peter S. Hawkins, *Dante's Testaments: Essays in Scriptural Imagination* (Stanford: Stanford University Press, 1999), 78, 86.

authority, or whether readers of poetry are inclined to grant this claim is a question for another day.

I want to finish this consideration of Williams's literary criticism by suggesting some lines of further enquiry. I think it would be worth pulling together and expounding his ideas on Shakespeare, Milton, Wordsworth and possibly also Coventry Patmore, who influenced him both as a poet and in his Romantic Theology. The mutually respectful but rather wary relationship that Williams had with Eliot would also be worth exploring.[97] Even more worthwhile, but very difficult, would be a presentation of Williams's poetics, the task which Mary McDermot Shideler shied from.[98] I think Dorothy Sayers could have done it, and she has given pointers in some of her essays. Meanwhile I commend this body of work to you, which, despite its flaws, provides a consideration of poetry mainly English which is both passionate and illuminating.

---

97. See the present writer's 'Charles Williams and T. S. Eliot: friends and rivals.'
98. The present writer's 'Metaphysical and Romantic in the Taliessin poems' attempts some aspects of this.

WILLIAMS AND LEWIS ON CO-INHERENCE

This book[1] explores the relationship between Williams and Lewis, not in personal terms, but through their literary work and their mutual influence. This covers the whole range of their writing, notably fiction, literary criticism, theology and, in Williams's case, poetry. Fiddes is well qualified for this: he took degrees in both theology and English literature, is ordained, is professor of systematic theology at Oxford and has written on both theology and literature. He has also been reading both Williams and Lewis since he was a child in the 1950s, and this book is based on a thorough knowledge of their works, with lesser use of the burgeoning secondary literature about both writers. Moreover, he has drawn on the archive of Raymond Hunt, who transcribed many lectures and other material by Williams.

The book is divided into four parts. The first charts the beginning of their friendship, their time together in Oxford during the War, and the continuing influence of Williams on Lewis after his death in 1945. The second part examines in detail the concept of co-inherence, when and from where Williams derived it and how he understood it, with an exploration of its influence on Lewis. The third part, which I found particularly interesting, considers Williams's understanding of romantic love as expressed in his Arthurian poems and takes issue with some of Lewis's interpretations of them. The fourth part studies Williams in relation to William Blake, Karl Barth and his own novels, then Lewis in relation to his own *Perelandra* and Thomas Traherne. There is a final part on the theology of co-inherence.

---

1. Paul S. Fiddes, *Charles Williams and C. S. Lewis: Friends in Co-inherence* (Oxford: Oxford University Press, 2021).

The book is tightly argued, and I can touch on only a few themes. Lewis and Williams first made contact in 1936, when Lewis wrote to congratulate Williams on his novel *The Place of the Lion*, which he had just read. Williams replied, praising Lewis for his scholarly work *The Allegory of Love*, which he had been seeing through the press, and saying: 'I regard your book as practically the only one that I have ever come across, since Dante, that shows the slightest understanding of what this very peculiar identity of love and religion means.' Lewis replied: 'I nowhere commit myself to a definite approval of this blend of erotic and religious feeling.'[2] He considered that he and Williams dwelt in 'quite distinct, though neighbouring' provinces 'in the country of Romance.' (His aversion from this theme perhaps accounts for the omission of a chapter on Dante in *The Allegory of Love*.) In fact, although Williams had described courtly love as 'very peculiar,' it was in fact one of his deepest convictions. It derived from his reading of Dante and his interpretation of the role of Beatrice. He had a sacramental understanding of sexual union, and also a belief that unconsummated unions could generate energy unavailable any other way. This accounts for the sexual games, which Fiddes rightly says are inexcusable, which Williams played with some of the young women who looked up to him. To be fair, Lewis also extolled a kind of sexual game in which the male is the sky-father and the female the earth-mother. However, Lewis urged an analogy whereas Williams saw an identity. This is at the heart of the difference between them. Lewis summed it up by quoting Denis de Rougemont: 'Eros ceases to be a demon only when he ceases to be a god,' which he did in a review of 1940[3] and later paraphrased in *The Four Loves*, near the end of his life.[4]

The term co-inherence, always spelled thus by Williams, he took from G. L Prestige's 1938 study, *God in Patristic Thought*, which became a standard work. Prestige uses this to refer to the relationship of the three Persons of the Trinity to one another, and it translates the Greek *perichoresis* and the Latin *circumincessio*. Williams uses it to convey the concept that all human beings are connected with one another and with God, and that all persons are dependent upon one another. Fiddes grants that these ideas are pervasive in all Williams's work but points out that he did not actually start using the term until 1939, notably in *The Descent of the Dove*. He suggests that Williams did not take this concept far enough, and that if we combine the insight that the lover is both bearer and born of a love that is Christ and that the lover shares in the eternal glory of Christ, this should bring us to the idea that the one who loves participates in eternal relations within the Trinity. He also develops a complex argument,

---

2. Williams, letter to Lewis, 12 March 1936; Lewis, letter to Williams, 23 March 1936, in Grevel Lindop, *Charles Williams: The Third Inkling* (London: Oxford University Press, 2015), 256, 259.
3. C.S. Lewis, review of Denis de Rougemont, *Passion and Society* (London: Faber, 1940), and Claude Chavasse, *The Bride of Christ* (London: Faber, 1940), *Theology* 20, no. 240 (June 1940): 459–461. Reprinted in Lewis, *Image and Imagination*, ed. by Walter Hooper (Cambridge: Cambridge University Press, 2013), 59–62 though the de Rougemont title is incorrectly listed as *Poetry and Society*.
4. C.S. Lewis, *The Four Loves* (London: Geoffrey Bles, 1960), 15.

which I am not sure that I accept, that Williams's ideas about exchange derive partly from his study of the Kabbala, in particular because the stations on the Sephirotic tree are linked by paths facilitating movement among them, though he should have cited A. E. Waite, Williams's source, rather than a modern scholar. Lewis, on the other hand, he suggests, was influenced not by the Kabbala but by Neoplatonism and in particular by the ideas of hierarchy, strict obedience and a sharp distinction between human love and divine glory, shown by an analysis of *That Hideous Strength*.

Williams admired Karl Barth's influential commentary, *The Epistle to the Romans*, and Fiddes has found notes of a lecture he gave on Barth. Williams seized on Barth's phrase 'impossible possibility,' which Barth used in relation to many aspects of faith. Fiddes notes that these are all positive, whereas Williams had used the same idea both positively, with the Beatrician moment, in which the beloved is seen as if unfallen, and negatively, as when Shakespeare's Troilus confronts the reality of Cressida's betrayal. Fiddes summarises the positive aspect in these words: 'The "impossible possibility" happens because there is co-inherence of God and humanity, centred on the birth of Christ in the human soul.'

I pass over Fiddes' discussion of Williams's novels to consider his study of Lewis's *Perelandra*, and, in particular, the Great Dance at the end of it. In the dance, every participant is at the centre, and Fiddes notes the derivation of this from the medieval saying, used by Bonaventure, that 'God is an intelligible sphere whose centre is everywhere and circumference nowhere.' Fiddes considers Lewis took this from Williams's *He Came Down from Heaven* and combined it with the ancient picture of the whole cosmos as a dance, as expounded by Lewis in *The Discarded Image*. However, Williams got there first with his image of the dance around the still point in his novel *The Greater Trumps*. (T. S. Eliot also used this image in *Burnt Norton*.) In *The Greater Trumps* the Fool at the centre of the dance also moves, though only one character, Sibyl, can see that. For Lewis, too, 'God is not a static *thing*' but 'almost a kind of dance.'[5] Lewis also appealed to the image of the dance in *The Problem of Pain* and *A Preface to Paradise Lost*, so for him it was more than a literary trope.

Lewis once wrote that Traherne's *Centuries* was 'almost the most beautiful book (in prose, I mean, excluding poets) in English,' but he never made more than brief mentions of it.[6] Nevertheless, Fiddes contends that Traherne is a persistent influence on Lewis because they shared a desire for something unknown. But they differed in where this was to be found. For Lewis, joy was 'an unsatisfied desire which is itself more desirable than any other satisfaction.'[7] He argued that the most probable explanation of this was that we were made for another world. For Traherne too, eternity is the object of every person's desire, but it can be

---

5. C.S. Lewis, *Beyond Personality: The Christian Idea of God* (New York: Macmillan, 1945), 21–22.
6. C.S. Lewis, letter to Arthur Greeves, 23 December 1941, *Collected Letters* ed. Walter Hooper (London: HarperCollins, 2000-2006), II, 505; quoted by Fiddes, 338.
7. C.S. Lewis, *Surprised by Joy* (London: Geoffrey Bles, 1955), 23–24; quoted by Fiddes, 340.

found in this world if you can only see it aright. He does not use the word co-inherence but Fiddes argues that he means the same thing by his own word In-being.

I have some quibbles. Fiddes tends to quote other authors from editions not available to Williams or Lewis. This makes no difference in the case of Blake, but it does for Malory, where he uses the Vinaver edition based on the Winchester manuscript rather than the rather different Pollard one based on Caxton, the only one known to Williams and the one Lewis preferred. He misquotes the title of Coleridge's *Biographia Literaria* and says, wrongly, that Williams did not read any of Coleridge's prose, overlooking the definition of symbol at the beginning of *The Figure of Beatrice* which, as Williams says, comes from Coleridge (*The Statesman's Manual*). The time lapse in *The Winter's Tale* is sixteen years, not twenty, and Fiddes misquotes Troilus' crucial line to Ulysses in Shakespeare's play. I am not wholly convinced by Fiddes' main thesis, that the idea of co-inherence was a link between Williams and Lewis. Nevertheless, this is a valuable book. I hope that someone will also work on the Raymond Hunt material and turn it into publishable form.

CHARLES WILLIAMS AND DANTE STUDIES IN ENGLAND IN THE TWENTIETH CENTURY

Much of the credit for popularizing Dante in England in the twentieth century must go to Charles Williams and to three other writers, all of whom were friends of his, though not necessarily of one another. These three were T. S. Eliot, C. S. Lewis and Dorothy L. Sayers. Only one of them, Lewis, was an academic, and he, though a medievalist, was not a Dante specialist. He may have been the only one who could read Italian without the help of a facing translation. In their critical works they all wrote for audiences whose primary concern was English literature and they all made it clear that they thought that readers of English literature should also come to terms with Dante, even if they had been initially put off. As Sayers put it: 'after all, fourteen thousand lines are fourteen thousand lines, especially if they are full of Guelfs and Ghibellines and Thomas Aquinas.'[1]

It is worth considering the state of Dante studies in England in the 1920s, when Eliot and Williams started writing about him. Britain had produced a number of fine Dante scholars, notably Edward Moore (1835-1916), Paget Toynbee (1855-1932) and Edmund Gardner (1865-1935). Moore produced the first complete edition of Dante's works in the original language, the Oxford Dante, in 1894, and published a series of *Studies in Dante* (1896-1917), which were a standard reference for a long time. Toynbee published a *Concise Dictionary of Proper Names and Notable Matters in the Works of Dante* (1914) which again became a scholarly resource, and Gardner published numerous studies on Dante. However, these were nearly all works for specialists. English readers of the *Comedy* (the word *Divine* was not part of Dante's title but was contributed by Boccaccio) who had no Italian tended to rely on Henry Francis

---

1. Dorothy L. Sayers, '...And telling you a Story,' *Further Papers on Dante*, London: Methuen, 1957, 1.

Cary's translation into Miltonic blank verse with the title *The Vision of Dante Alighieri* (1805-1814). This had been praised by Coleridge and Wordsworth and it continued to be reprinted well into the twentieth century. For the *Vita Nuova* or *Nova* the standard version was the 1861 one by Dante Gabriel Rossetti in *The Early Italian Poets*, again frequently reprinted.

However, for those who were prepared to engage with the Italian, there was a resource which was widely read for many years and which was used by all four of the writers here. This was the Temple Classics edition of Dante's works. This was put together by a team under the leadership of Philip Wicksteed between 1899 and 1906. As well as the *Comedy* in three volumes and the *Vita Nuova and Canzoniere* in one, each containing Italian texts and English prose translations on facing pages, there were also English only versions of the *Convivio* and the *Latin Works*. A companion volume reprinted Rossetti's *Early Italian Poets*, which meant that both prose and verse versions of the *Vita Nuova* were available.

Eliot started to read Dante while a student at Harvard in 1908.[2] The influence was strong and immediate. His first acknowledged poem, *The Love Song of J. Alfred Prufrock*, begun in 1909, begins with an epigraph from Dante. His most influential poem, *The Waste Land*, published in 1922, has several allusions to Dante, with the references given in his notes. Meanwhile he wrote about Dante in prose. His first essay on him appeared initially in a magazine and then in his first prose collection, *The Sacred Wood*, 1920. The first thing to note about this is that there was an essay on Dante at all in a book otherwise about English writers, though it did have a few glances at French critics. In it, Eliot is concerned to demonstrate that "philosophical" poetry—he uses quotation marks—is a legitimate form. However, he then sidesteps the issue of the philosophy Dante undoubtedly incorporated into the *Comedy* to consider the issue of the allegory which gives his poem its structure. He says:

> Sometimes the philosophy is confused with the allegory. The philosophy is an ingredient, it is a part of Dante's world just as it is a part of life; the allegory is the scaffold on which the poem is built. . . It is not essential that the allegory or the almost unintelligible astronomy should be understood—only that its presence should be justified. The emotional structure within this scaffold is what must be understood—the structure made possible by the scaffold. This structure is an ordered scale of human emotions. . . Dante's is the most comprehensive, and the most ordered presentation of emotions that has ever been made.[3]

---

2. Robert Crawford, *Young Eliot: from St Louis to The Waste Land* (London: Jonathan Cape, 2015), 118. Eliot's own reminiscences are in 'What Dante means to me,' *To Criticize the Critic* (London: Faber, 1965), 125-135.

3. Eliot, *The Sacred Wood* (London: Methuen, 1950), 163, 168 (also in T. S. Eliot, *The Collected Prose*, III, Baltimore: Johns Hopkins University Press, 2015, 228, 231). This is a reprint of the 1928 edition, to which Eliot added a Preface. The text of the Dante essay was not changed. The astronomical notes in the Temple Classics edition are, indeed, extremely terse as Sayers was later to complain. Eliot could have consulted M. A. Orr's *Dante and the Early Astronomers* (London: Gall and Inglis, 1913), which explains the astronomical references clearly.

Eliot's caution here is notable. He was writing for an audience which, as far as Dante's faith was concerned, would have included sceptics, adherents of other faiths or of none, and staunch Protestants who would have been suspicious of Dante as a medieval Catholic. He himself was only some way on a faith journey which led into his reception into the Church of England in 1927. In effect, what he is saying here is that you can appreciate Dante while ignoring his beliefs.

The issue of whether and to what extent you need to share a poet's beliefs to appreciate him continued to preoccupy Eliot. The issue was brought up by I. A. Richards in an article for Eliot's magazine, *The Criterion*, later reprinted in his little book *Science and Poetry*. Praising Eliot's own poem, *The Waste Land*, Richards said that Eliot:

> by effecting a complete separation between his poetry and *all* beliefs, and this without any weakening of the poetry, has realised what might otherwise have remained largely a speculative possibility.[4]

This led to a dialogue between Eliot and Richards which continued for a few years. In an article in 1927 Eliot took up Richards' comment on *The Waste Land*, saying 'I cannot for the life of me see the "complete separation" from all belief,' and went on more generally to affirm:

> I cannot see that poetry can ever be separated from something which I should call belief, and to which I cannot see any reason for refusing the name of belief, unless we are to reshuffle names altogether.[5]

Shortly afterwards Eliot reviewed *Science and Poetry*, and here he raised the issue of Dante, asking:

> what right have we to assert what Dante actually believed, or how he believed it? Did he believe in the *Summa* as St. Thomas believed in it, and did even St. Thomas believe in it as M. Maritain does?[6]

Eliot was to return to the issue in his short book on Dante, but meanwhile we turn to Williams. We don't know exactly when he started reading Dante, but it must have been before 1911, when he made excerpts from Rossetti's translation of the *Vita Nuova* in his Arthurian

---

4. Richards, *Science and Poetry* (London: Kegan Paul, 1926), 64-5.
5. Eliot, 'A Note on Poetry and Belief,' *The Enemy*, 1 (Jan. 1927), 15-17, also in *The Complete Prose*, III, 18-20.
6. Eliot, 'Literature, Science, and Dogma: A review of *Science and Poetry*, by I. A. Richards,' *The Dial*, 82 (Mar 1927) [239]-243, reprinted in T. S. Eliot, *The Complete Prose*, III, 44-48.

notebook.[7] And we know that his introduction to the *Comedy* came through reading proofs of a reprint of Cary's translation, as he later told Dorothy Sayers.[8] Sayers also recorded his reaction to the reading, which was 'But this is *true*.' This is very different from the caution with which Eliot expressed himself about Dante's beliefs. This was not only because the two men had very different temperaments, but partly also because Eliot was in the process of finding faith, whereas Williams was a cradle Anglican.

Furthermore, there were some similarities and some differences in their experience of love. After all, the main inspiration for both the *Vita Nuova* and the *Comedy* was Dante's continuing love for Beatrice, whom he first saw as a child, who as an adult married someone else, and who died young. Eliot's relationship with Vivienne Haigh-Wood, whom he married on impulse, was not this kind.[9] That with Emily Hale possibly was; he carried on a long flirtation with her which eventually led nowhere. Eliot's later friendship with Mary Trevelyan and his second marriage, to Valerie Fletcher, were not of the idealizing kind. But for Williams this was exactly the kind of love that he had felt not once, but twice, first with Florence Conway, who became his wife, and then with Phyllis Jones, his second love, though this relationship was never consummated.[10] These were formative experiences for him, and led to his development of what he called his romantic theology. This was, in brief, the idea that romantic love was a religious experience and a way to the divine but was undervalued by the church.

Williams seems to have first seen this idea clearly expressed in the poetry of Coventry Patmore, notably the poems in his collection *To the Unknown Eros* and his prose work, *The Rod, The Root and the Flower*. He incorporated it in his early poems, such as the sonnet sequence *The Silver Stair* (written by 1910) and in the 1920s started working out his ideas about idealizing love in a short book, *Outlines of Romantic Theology*. By then he had read and absorbed Dante, and in it he says:

> It is certain that the genius of Dante first showed us what may be called the religious spirit in Love. By the writings of Dante and of minds like his the rest of us have been made aware of the profundities which are concealed in this fastidious and passionate devotion; for phrases which might be used, as it were colloquially, by any lover, take on a sudden significance when used by these men, and we become aware that we do not excusably exaggerate in saying, for example,

---

7. Grevel Lindop, *Charles Williams: The Third Inkling* (Oxford: Oxford University Press, 2015), 43.
8. Dorothy L. Sayers, *The Poetry of Search and the Poetry of Statement* (London: Victor Gollancz, 1963), 73.
9. See Carole Seymour Jones, *Painted Shadow: a Life of Vivienne Eliot* (London: Constable, 2001). For Emily Hale, see Lyndall Gordon, *The Hyacinth Girl: T. S. Eliot's hidden Muse* (London: Virago, 2022). For Mary Trevelyan see Mary Trevelyan and Erica Wagner, *Mary and Mr Eliot: a Sort of Love Story* (London: Faber, 2022). For Valerie Fletcher and Eliot's life generally, see Robert Crawford, *Young Eliot: from St Louis to The Waste Land*, and *Eliot after The Waste Land* (London: Jonathan Cape, 2015 and 2022).
10. See Lindop, *Charles Williams*, who deals with this extensively.

"It's heaven to be with her," but on the contrary express without perhaps realising it an eternal and immortal truth.[11]

However, this book, which would have provided a public treatment of belief in Dante contrary to that of Eliot, had an unfortunate history. Williams completed it probably in 1924, submitted it first to Humphrey Milford, his own employer at the London branch of the Oxford University Press, who rejected it, then to the Nonesuch Press and then again to the new firm of Faber and Gwyer. It was read there by Osbert Burdett, an appropriate reader to choose, as he was an authority on Coventry Patmore.[12] (Eliot had only just joined the firm and had not yet established his religious position.) Burdett said *Outlines* was 'beautifully written' but delayed a decision on publishing it and finally asked Williams to expand and resubmit it the following year. However, Williams did not revise or resubmit the book, and it was published only long after his death.[13]

We return to Eliot and his short book called simply *Dante*. This came out in 1929; it was incorporated in Eliot's 1932 *Selected Essays*, but the separate publication remained in print for many years and *Selected Essays* is still current. I pass over his skilful account of the *Comedy*, which is designed to attract readers who might be hesitant about the philosophy, religion or need for annotation, to return to the issue of belief. Eliot says:

> My point is that you cannot afford to ignore Dante's philosophical and theological beliefs, or to skip the passages which express them most clearly; but that you are not called upon to believe them yourself.[14]

And Eliot attached a Note to this part of his book which continued to worry away at the issue of poetry and belief without reaching any firm conclusion. However, in his discussion of the *Vita Nuova*, he comes much closer to the position of Williams about the significance of Beatrice to Dante, though in his own typically cautious and guarded way:

> The *Vita Nuova* . . . is a mixture of biography and allegory; but a mixture according to a recipe not available to the modern mind . . . I find in it an account of a particular kind of experience: that is, of something which had actual experience (the experience of the 'confession' in the modern sense) and intellectual and imaginative experience (the experience of thought and the experience of dream) as its materials; and which became a third kind. . . . If you have that sense of

---

11. Charles Williams, *Outlines of Romantic Theology* (Grand Rapids: Wm. B Eerdmans, 1990), 56.
12. His study, *The Idea of Coventry Patmore*, had been published by the Oxford University Press in 1921.
13. On the vicissitudes of *Outlines of Romantic Theology*, see Alice Mary Hadfield, Introduction to *Outlines*, and Lindop, *Charles Williams*, 108-112, 121-123, 143.
14. Eliot, *Selected Essays*, third edition (London: Faber, 1951), 257, also in *The Complete Prose*, III, 717.

intellectual and spiritual realities that Dante had, then a form of expression like the *Vita Nuova* cannot be classed either as 'truth' or 'fiction.'[15]

By this time Eliot had achieved a considerable reputation, thanks to his poetry, particularly *The Waste Land*, his critical essays, his editorship of the literary periodical *The Criterion* and the patronage he was able to offer younger poets at what had become Faber and Faber. He was still regarded as a modernist, thanks to his announcement of himself as a classicist and his repudiation of Milton and the Romantic poets. Eliot's continued championing of Dante therefore carried considerable weight among poets and students of English literature.

I come next to Lewis and his 1936 study *The Allegory of Love*, the book which made his reputation. This is a survey of allegorical medieval poems which embody the idea of courtly love, which Lewis says has four distinctive marks: Humility, Courtesy, Adultery, and the Religion of Love.[16] He traces this from late Roman poetry to medieval France, where a key text is the *Roman de la Rose*, begun by Guillaume de Lorris and completed, at great length, by Jean de Meun. After a sympathetic discussion, he suggests that Jean could not unify his poem, and he concludes this with a comparison with Dante, worth quoting at length:

> All Jean's ideas were in themselves capable of fusion, but he could not fuse them. The nature and extent of his failure become clear as soon as we think of Dante. Odd as it may sound, it is none the less true that the materials of the two poets are very nearly the same. It is almost true to say that there was nothing in Dante which was not also in Jean de Meun—except Dante himself. In both we find the same starting point—courtly love: in both the same stores of scholastic learning and the same determination to impart them: the same unfettered range of heterogenous experiences, both actual and imagined. If it is said that they differ in merely technical power, I reply that technique is itself only one manifestation of the unifying faculty. The power which welds raw masses of experience into a whole is the same which, in the single phrase, elicits from the chaos of language the perfect words and the perfect syntactical device. Thus, in a sense Jean lacked nothing which Dante had, except the power to co-ordinate. But that exception is fatal. Because of it, Dante remains a strong candidate for the supreme poetical honours of the world, while Jean de Meun is read only by professional scholars, and not by very many of them.[17]

Of course, that final phrase begs the question as to how widely Dante is read, but let that pass, along with the issue of whether this is a fair judgement of Jean de Meun. I can at least attest that this passage led one reader many years ago to read the *Comedy*. It is this which

---

15. *Selected Essays*, 272-3; *Complete Prose*, III, 731.
16. C. S. Lewis, *The Allegory of Love* (Oxford: Oxford University Press, 1936), 12.
17. Lewis, *Allegory of Love*, 154-5.

leads me to include Lewis as an effective popularizer of Dante. However, more to the point is that Lewis, rather surprisingly, did not follow this up with a whole chapter on the *Vita Nuova* and the *Comedy*, but instead gives the remaining chapters of the book to works in English, from Chaucer to Spenser.

One would have expected the *Comedy* to be a key text for Lewis. Dante's idealizing love for Beatrice was the subject of the *Vita Nuova*, and in the *Comedy* it is Beatrice who sends Virgil to rescue Dante from the dark wood at the opening of *Inferno*, who later appears to him near the end of *Purgatorio* and who guides him in the *Paradiso*. This is surely the most extended and developed example of courtly love in all literature, and it is worth considering why Lewis did not choose to discuss it in detail.

Now, it was Williams who had the task of seeing Lewis's book through the publication process, and he wrote enthusiastically to Lewis about it. He said: 'I regard your book as practically the only one I have ever come across, since Dante, that shows the slightest understanding of what this very peculiar identity of love and religion means.' In his reply Lewis repudiated the idea that he might have accepted this himself, saying: 'I think you will find that I nowhere commit myself to a definite approval of this blend of erotic and religious feeling.'[18] It seems a strange thing to say, but I rather wonder whether this is why Lewis shied away from offering a detailed discussion of what would have been the culminating exemplar of his thesis. He does indeed say that in the *Comedy* 'the quarrel between Christianity and the love religion was made up.'[19]

It is worth pausing and noting Lewis's reasons for repudiating the religion of love, the idealizing kind of love which Dante had for Beatrice, despite having written about other examples of it. He explained this a few years later, in a discussion, not of Dante but of Shelley, and specifically of his poem *Epipsychidion*. In it, Shelley addresses a young Italian woman in terms so idealized as practically to deify her:

> Seraph of Heaven! too gentle to be human,
> Veiling beneath that radiant form of Woman
> All that is insupportable in thee
> Of light, and love, and immortality!
> Veiled glory of this lampless Universe!
> Thou Moon beyond the clouds! Thou living Form
> Among the Dead! Thou Star above the Storm!
> (*Epipsychidion*, 21-8)

---

18. Williams, letter to Lewis, 12 March 1936; Lewis, letter to Williams, 23 March 1936, in Lindop, *Charles Williams*, 256, 259. This exchange led to their friendship.
19. Lewis, *Allegory of Love*, 23.

There is a great deal more in the same vein. Shelley prefaces his poem with a number of Dantean references. Here is Lewis's criticism of *Epipsychidion*, and therefore of this whole kind of idealizing love:

> I think the thought implied in [*Epipsychidion*] a dangerous delusion. In it Shelley is trying to stand on a particular rung of the Platonic ladder, and I happen to believe firmly that that particular rung does not exist, and that the man who thinks he is standing on it is not standing but falling . . . There is an element of spiritual, and also of carnal, passion in it, each expressed with great energy and sensibility, and the whole is marred, but not completely, by the false mode . . . in which the poet tries to blend them.[20]

The Platonic ladder is the process Plato described in the *Symposium*, whereby a lover moves from sexual desire for a particular individual through various stages to the love of absolute beauty. However, this process is very similar to Williams's romantic theology, and it shows Williams to be in opposition to Lewis, as he had been to Eliot, this time on the significance of the Beatrician experience.

I cannot leave Lewis without returning to his admiration for Dante and his thinking about love. He later published three scholarly articles on Dante, though not on Dante's treatment of love,[21] and there is also a revealing aside in his discussion of Williams's Arthurian poems. He is considering the issue of obscurity in them and compares it to that in Eliot's *The Waste Land*. He goes on to say:

> If you have never read Dante or Shakespeare certain things in that poem will be obscure to you. But then, frankly, we ought to have read Dante and Shakespeare; or at least the poet has a right to address only those who have done so.[22]

Lewis's final thoughts on love come in one of his last books, *The Four Loves*. Here, he gives a chapter to Eros, sexual love, including the idealizing love which is at issue here. Here he says:

> Eros, honoured without reservation and obeyed unconditionally, becomes a demon . . . Years ago when I wrote about medieval love-poetry and described its strange, half make-believe, "reli-

---

20. C. S. Lewis, 'Shelley, Dryden and Mr Eliot', in *Selected Literary Essays* (Cambridge: Cambridge University Press 1969), 203. This essay was first published in 1939.
21. They are collected in his *Studies in Medieval and Renaissance Literature* (Cambridge: Cambridge University Press, 1966).
22. Charles Williams and C. S. Lewis, *Arthurian Torso*, Oxford: Oxford University Press, 1948, 189.

gion of love," I was blind enough to treat this as an almost purely literary phenomenon. I know better now. Eros by his nature invites it.[23]

We return to Williams and to his mature work on Dante. In 1939 he praised a new translation of the *Comedy* by John D. Sinclair, which, like the Temple Classics version, had a prose translation facing the Italian, but in a larger format, better notes, and a commentary chapter following each canto.[24] Although first published by another publisher, it was later taken up by the Oxford University Press and largely displaced the Temple Classics version for students of the next generation. Then in 1941 Williams published a pamphlet, *Religion and Love in Dante: the Theology of Romantic Love*,[25] and finally in 1943 *The Figure of Beatrice: a Study in Dante*. This was commissioned by Eliot, with whom Williams had become on friendly terms, and published by Faber and Faber. By this time Williams was at the height of his reputation, thanks to his novels, his Arthurian poems and his teaching at Oxford in war time. The book was favourably reviewed and widely read. It is the best of Williams's critical works and also embodies the best exposition of his view of idealizing romantic love, which by this time he had generalized into the Way of Affirmation of Images. Of this he saw Dante as the greatest record.[26] In it he says that what Dante saw in Beatrice is an experience common to lovers and he explains its significance in this way:

> The immediate suggestion . . . is that what Dante sees is the glory of Beatrice as she is 'in heaven'—that is, as God chose her, unfallen, original; or (if better) redeemed; but at least, either way, celestial. What he sees is something real. It is not 'realer' than the actual Beatrice who, no doubt, had many serious faults, but it is as real. Both Beatrices are aspects of one Beatrice. The revealed virtues are real; so is the celestial beauty. The divinely intelligent angel is quite right; the place of this heavenly creature is heaven.[27]

In fact the book can be seen not simply as a commentary on Dante but as the fullest exposition of Williams's Way of Affirmation of Images, using Dante to illustrate it. However, I have had my say about this book elsewhere[28] so I shall simply cite Williams's first biographer, Alice Mary Hadfield, on its three themes: 'the way of affirmation of images as man's way to

---

23. C. S Lewis, *The Four Loves* (London: Geoffrey Bles, 1960), 127.
24. Dante, *The Divine Comedy, Inferno* and *Purgatorio*, London: The Bodley Head, 1939. (*Paradiso* was to follow in 1946.) Williams's review is 'Men and Books,' *Time and Tide* XX (June 24, 1939): 833-4. In *The Figure of Beatrice* he cites both the Temple and the Sinclair versions.
25. London: The Dacre Press, 1941. It has been reprinted both in Williams, *Outlines of Romantic Theology* and in Charles Williams, *The Celian Moment and Other Essays* (Carterton: The Greystones Press, 2017).
26. Charles Williams, *The Figure of Beatrice* (London: Faber, 1943), 11.
27. Williams, *The Figure of Beatrice*, 27.
28. See 'Charles Williams as a Literary Critic.'

God, the way of romantic love as a particular mode of the same, and the involution of this love with images of the community or City, with poetry and human learning.'[29]

One reader on whom *The Figure of Beatrice* had a great effect was Dorothy L. Sayers, who recorded that she read it 'not because it was about Dante, but because it was by Charles Williams.'[30] She took down the Temple Classics edition and found that Dante 'was simply the most incomparable story-teller who ever set pen to paper.'[31] She embarked on an enthusiastic correspondence with Williams as she worked her way through the *Comedy*. This is reprinted in the third volume of her *Letters* and makes delightful reading. I shall quote just one sentence; on finishing reading the *Inferno*, about how Dante managed to make damnation exciting, she wrote: 'To anybody who can write 34 cantos of about 140 lines apiece on a subject like that and keep you worked up all the time I take off 34 hats one after the other.'[32]

She formed the idea of translating the *Comedy* in collaboration with Williams, but he died before this plan got anywhere. She went ahead on her own, and completed and published *Hell* and *Purgatory* (she used English titles) in the Penguin Classics series, in 1949 and 1955. She died while working on *Paradise*, which was completed in 1962 by her friend Barbara Reynolds, who later wrote a charming study about the whole project.[33] Sayers translated the poem into *terza rima*, the verse form Dante used, and dismissed the alleged difficulties of writing *terza rima* in English, pointing to the example of a contemporary poem in this metre.[34] She provided extensive introductions and notes. She dedicated her work to Williams, as 'the dead master of the affirmations,' and acknowledged her debt to him in her Introductions and frequently in her commentaries. She also dealt with the issue of belief which so troubled Eliot by explaining simply and clearly the doctrines involved and, as she was a skilled Christian apologist,[35] doing so convincingly.

These Penguin Classics volumes were kept in print for many years and undoubtedly introduced many people to the *Comedy* who might otherwise have been daunted. C. S. Lewis provided a fair summing up of their qualities:

---

29. Alice Mary Hadfield, *Charles Williams: An Exploration of his Life and Work* (Oxford: Oxford University Press, 1983), 209.
30. '...And telling you a Story,' 1.
31. ibid. 2.
32. Dorothy L. Sayers, *Letters III: 1944-1950: A Noble Daring* (Cambridge: The Dorothy L. Sayers Society, 1998), 48.
33. Barbara Reynolds, *The Passionate Intellect: Dorothy L. Sayers' Encounter with Dante* (Kent: Kent State University Press), 1989.
34. Louis MacNeice, *Autumn Sequel* (London: Faber, 1953).
35. Sayers' apologetic works were *The Mind of the Maker* (London: Methuen, 1941), *Unpopular Opinions* (London: Gollancz, 1946), *Creed or Chaos?* (London: Methuen, 1947) and *The Christ of the Creeds* (Hustpierpoint: Dorothy L Sayers Society, 2008). Articles from the first of three of these were collected as *Letters to a Diminished Church* (Nashville: W Publishing Group, 2004).

I suppose we are not all agreed as to the two characteristics of Dorothy Sayers's own Dante. One eminently laudable is the apparatus. No doubt there are some errors: but as a whole, it is a model of judicious popularisation which has already proved useful to thousands. Such work was never more needed than now and is in very short supply.

The other characteristic is more controversial. As a translator Dorothy Sayers is the arch-rebel against the Cary tradition. It had represented Dante as an earlier Milton. She discovered for herself Dante as the exciting story-teller, the writer of high comedy, even the writer of low farce.

Nor is there the least doubt that the very un-Miltonic qualities she saw in Dante are really there. The question is whether her reading of Dante did not exaggerate them or whether the colloquialism and comically violent rhythms by which she tried to represent them did not carry the exaggeration further.[36]

As well as her translation, I should also mention Sayers' essays on Dante, which were also addressed to non-specialist readers.[37]

It was really Sayers who completed the work begun by Eliot and Williams, and hinted at by Lewis, by putting into the hands of ordinary readers, at a modest price, a version of the *Comedy* in a readable translation and with helpful notes.

I end with Eliot, who provided a personal tribute to Dante in his later years. I pass over his account of Dante's influence on him as a poet, to note that his final tribute, like his earlier one, is not to the storytelling or the doctrines and the issue of poetry and belief which had so vexed him, but to that of emotion:

> The Divine Comedy expresses everything in the way of emotion, between depravity's despair and the beatific vision, that man is capable of experiencing. It is therefore a constant reminder to the poet, of the obligation to explore, to find words for the inarticulate, to capture those feelings which people can hardly even feel, because they have no words for them; and at the same time, a reminder that the explorer beyond the frontiers of ordinary consciousness will only be able to return and report to his fellow-citizens, if he has all the time a firm grasp of the realities with which they are already acquainted.[38]

---

36. C. S. Lewis, 'Rhyme and Reason: Dorothy L. Sayers, *The Poetry of Search and the Poetry of Statement*,' *Image and Imagination* (Cambridge: Cambridge University Press, 2013), 237-8.
37. *Introductory Papers on Dante* (London: Methuen, 1954); *Further Papers on Dante* (London: Methuen, 1957); *The Poetry of Search and the Poetry of Statement* (London: Gollancz, 1963). All three have been reprinted in recent years by Wipf and Stock.
38. T. S. Eliot, 'What Dante means to me,' *To Criticize the Critic*, (London Faber,1965), 134, also in *The Complete Prose*, VII, 482-490.

In their work of popularisation, something which has been largely ignored by professional Dante scholars, these four writers brought a medieval poem of fourteen thousand lines, full of Guelfs, Ghibellines and Thomas Aquinas, within the grasp of ordinary readers of their day, and they should be honoured for so doing.

THE REUNION OF DANTE AND BEATRICE

The musical critic Donald Tovey once said, 'a great artist's feeling is often most profound where his expression is most ornate,'[1] and one of the attractions of tackling the climax of the *Purgatorio* in Canto XXX is the combination of great depth of feeling with extreme elaboration of expression and great wealth of symbolism. Yet Dante manages to make his allegorical machinery carry all the necessary symbolism so that the actual reunion of Dante and Beatrice is a meeting of two people as well as the symbolic climax of this part of the whole work.

Dante and Beatrice meet, then, in the first instance, according to the conventions of courtly love. He was supposed to be her faithful lover, according to the convention which did not expect sexual fulfilment; he was not true to his faith; they are reunited, and she upbraids him for his unfaithfulness. All this is according to the convention, except that she took action to recover him, and it is not part of the convention for the lady to take such action. Whether love ever actually followed the convention, or whether it was a purely literary device, is not relevant here.[2] Dante assumed that readers understood the convention, and it is sufficiently close to the more recent sentiment to be easily understood today.

However, beneath this attractive but perhaps rather artificial convention lies some realistic psychology. And here Dante is very bold: he compares himself to a child wanting his mother both in his reaching out towards Virgil, now suddenly gone, and also in his relation

---

1. *Essays in Musical Analysis: Chamber Music* (Oxford: Oxford University Press, 1944), 132.
2. I am relying on the celebrated discussion by C. S. Lewis in *The Allegory of Love* Oxford: Oxford University Press, 1936), chapter 1.

to Beatrice, who tells him off thoroughly and publicly. This starts from, but goes beyond, the courtly love convention and beyond what the historical Dante would have expected from the historical Beatrice. The nearest similar point is her refusal of his salutation in *Vita Nuova* X, which caused him such grief, but this passage and the following one in *Purgatorio* draw also on his experience as a child and as a mature man.

But beyond this lies the significance which Beatrice had for him. We need to appreciate that in the *Vita Nuova* she seemed to him a divine being. This is the burden of the whole book, and incidentally the reason for its being, for a time, censored by the church. It is not uncommon for a young man or even a boy to see his lady as divine; where Dante was unusual was in seeing this as a genuine attribute of hers, and as requiring a theological explanation. This is hinted at throughout the *Vita Nuova*, particularly in the canzone 'Donne, ch'avete intelletto d'amore' ('Ladies that have intelligence in love' *Vita Nuova* XIX) and is fundamental to the *Commedia*. The theological explanation was set out by Charles Williams is that the lover sees the lady as the disciples saw Jesus at the Transfiguration, clothed in the Body of Glory that Christians believe the blessed will assume in Heaven. His fundamental response to seeing Beatrice in this way was not possession but adoration; of course there is an erotic element, but this is not primary, and it is for this reason, rather than because of the courtly love conventions, that marriage or sexual union is not the issue.

Now, when the Beatricean pageant is presented in *Purgatorio*, we are to understand that those taking part in it are presenting a show. The normal convention of the poem is that the characters in it, including Dante as a character, Virgil and Beatrice, are symbolic personages. They represent ideas, Dante as a representative man, Virgil as Reason or Nature, and Beatrice as Grace, but they carry these ideas through the continuous symbolism of the allegory and not in the straightforward way of the allegorical personifications we meet, for example, in Bunyan's *Pilgrim's Progress*, or the abstractions of pageants and official art.[3] However, in the pageant, those taking part are putting on a show in which they play parts. We can compare the allegorical masques which Shakespeare included in some of his late plays. Apart from Beatrice herself, those taking part in the pageant are angels or discarnate intelligences and are not otherwise characters in the poem.

In the previous canto Dante has made these allegorical personifications clear. We have the books of the Old and New Testaments, the cardinal and theological virtues and so on. But what is at the centre of the procession? The angels' cry of 'Benedictus qui venis' evokes both Palm Sunday where it greeted Jesus's entry into Jerusalem, and also the Canon of the Mass,

---

3. I am drawing on the distinction as set out by Dorothy L. Sayers: Dante, *Purgatory* translated Sayers (Harmondsworth: Penguin, 1955), 302.

where it is part of the consecration of the elements. Sinclair[4] argues that the pageant is in fact a Corpus Christi procession and that this should guide the interpretation.

Corpus Christi is the feast which celebrates the institution of the Eucharist and is a joyful counterpart to the celebration on Maundy Thursday, which is inevitably dominated by the Passion. It was first instituted by Pope Urban IV in 1261 and renewed by Pope John XXII in 1317, at the time Dante was working on *Purgatorio*. By the early fourteenth century it had become widely observed, and it had become customary to mount a procession. There was no fixed form for this, but at the centre was a canopy under which a priest carried the Host in a tabernacle or a monstrance.[5]

Beatrice therefore plays the part of the Host, that is, of Christ. The angels' cry is turned into the second person because they address her, while retaining the masculine gender because she plays this part. For Dante, she is the mediator of grace, not, of course, as an alternative to Jesus, Mary or the saints, but as a personal complement to them. When, in *Paradiso*, her mission has been accomplished, she returns to her place in the Celestial Rose and directs Dante's gaze upwards. We all may have equivalents to Beatrice—Charles Williams suggests that they may not necessarily even be people; for Wordsworth the mediator was wild nature —and I think this may be the point of Dante keeping Statius in the poem until the end of the cantica. We are to infer that he would have seen a vision appropriate to his personal experience.

As a mediator of grace, Beatrice supersedes Virgil. This is artistically necessary for the poem, but we need to understand that it is theologically necessary as well. The shock and grief we feel at the absence of Virgil is the shock of the Christian who is trying to lead the Christian life, being the old man on the new way, feeling the pull of all those natural, normal and indeed entirely admirable human affections and interests which for the poem are summed up in the figure of Virgil, but which Christians believe will in themselves take us no farther than Limbo.

Dante, with great boldness and confidence, emphasizes this. Over the longer term he does this through the increasing warmth of the relationship between Virgil and Dante, which of course has its allegorical significance as Dante the character's understanding of what he has seen and of Virgil's teaching increases, but also has the direct appeal of a growing friendship between master and pupil. In the passage under discussion, he goes further by including two direct quotations from the *Aeneid*. The first, at line 21, evokes the sorrow felt at the loss of Marcellus, and anticipates Dante's sorrow at the loss of Virgil himself. The second, at line 48, fuses Dido's memory of Sychaeus, her first husband who had been murdered, on seeing

---

4. Dante, *The Divine Comedy: Purgatorio* translated J. D. Sinclair (London: Bodley Head, 1939), *Purgatorio*, 415.
5. Miri Rubin, *Corpus Christi* (Cambridge: Cambridge University Press, 1991), 181 and 243-270. Unfortunately, Rubin does not mention Dante.

Aeneas with Dante's own memory of his early passion for Beatrice and it is with these words on his lips that Dante finds Virgil to be gone. Virgil had not prepared us for the sternness of Beatrice's greeting to Dante, which is consistent with the courtly love tradition as well as being supported by all the allegorical meanings, but which is nevertheless surprising and shocking. And her subsequent reproof, as well as carrying all the necessary meanings, also achieves artistically the one thing we would have thought impossible: we forget Virgil.[6]

The final point to make on the reunion of Dante and Beatrice, is that it is so convincing and real it is hard to remember that it is not a memory but a story; a vision, or, rather, a poem cast in the form of a vision. It never actually happened. We cannot know whether it corresponds to the vision Dante said he had at the end of the *Vita Nuova*, or whether that refers to the final vision at the end of *Paradiso*, but here in his exaltation of Beatrice he has fulfilled his promise to 'write concerning her what hath not before been written of any woman.'

---

6. Sayers, *Purgatory*, 26.

SOURCES AND ACKNOWLEDGEMENTS

Some of these essays have been published before and are reprinted by permission.

'Charles Williams and T. S. Eliot: friends and rivals' in *Journal of Inklings Studies* Vol. 9, No. 1 (April 2019)

'Metaphysical and romantic in the Taliessin poems' in *VII: An Anglo-American Literary Review* Vol. 20 ©2003 and is reprinted here with permission from the Marion E. Wade Center, Wheaton College, Wheaton, IL.

'Two books on the Holy Grail' in *Charles Williams Society Newsletter*, No. 113, Winter 2004

'Heraclitus and the Way of Exchange' in *Charles Williams Society Newsletter*, No. 112, Autumn 2004

'Williams and the sea nymph' in *Charles Williams Quarterly* No 119, Summer 2006

'A debt to George Eliot?' in *Charles Williams Society Newsletter* No. 116, Autumn 2005

'People and places in the Taliessin poems' in *Charles Williams Society Newsletter* No. 107 Summer 2003

'A note on the text of the Taliessin poems' in *VII: An Anglo-American Literary Review* Vol. 20 ©2003. See above.

'Thomas Howard on the novels' in *Charles Williams Society Newsletter* No. 32 Winter 1983

'Charles Williams as a father' in *Journal of Inklings Studies* Vol. 6, No. 1 (April 2016)

'Charles Williams as a literary critic' in *Charles Williams Quarterly* No. 133, Winter 2009

'Williams and Lewis on Co-inherence' in *Journal of Inklings Studies* Vol. 12, No. 2 (October 2022)

The other articles are unpublished though some have circulated in draft online.

The map for the Taliessin poems was prepared by Lynton Lamb under Williams's direction and included as an endpaper in the first edition of *Taliessin through Logres*, Oxford University Press, 1938. It is included here by permission of the Press.

www.ingramcontent.com/pod-product-compliance
Lightning Source LLC
Chambersburg PA
CBHW080323170426
43193CB00017B/2887